A Mother's Love

Bettyrose Woody

BettyRoseWoody@gmail.com

A Mother's Love

BETTYROSE WOODY

ISBN-13: 9781546376187
ISBN-10: 1546376186
Library of Congress Control Number: 2017907649
CreateSpace Independent Publishing Platform
North Charleston, South Carolina

Dedication

Books don't write themselves, and no author commits words to paper without the help and support of others. In my case, I have several notes of thanks to extend for the existence of this labor of love.

First, I want to thank my son Allen. He came into my life at the time I needed him most. He gave me permission to let my defenses down and open my heart. Through him I learned to love and to be loved without reservation.

Next, I want to thank my husband Joe for his gentleness, kindness, and unfailing love. I don't know what I'd do without all your love, help, and support. My life is richer for having you in it.

I also want to thank Tom McCarthy for helping me complete the manuscript. It was a labor of love for both of us. I will never forget all I learned from you.

I want to send a word of gratitude to my grandson Issac for being in my life and in my heart. I miss you so much, and hopefully, through the Grace of God, we will see each other again.

Last, but most importantly, I want to thank God. I spoke to him every day to get me through the tough times, and to share with Him the good times. My faith in Him brought me through and into the light. He saved me body and soul.

Bettyrose

One

AUSTELL, GEORGIA

Fassad's hands were huge, bigger than most men's, certainly much bigger than mine. You'd notice their size when he would reach out to shake a hand or pat someone on the back, which he often did. Fassad was nothing if not charming, at least to strangers.

His hands were what I noticed first when he put the pistol to his head. It was difficult not to, because my own right hand was wrapped helplessly around the pistol inside his clenched fists.

Fassad was a strong man given to unpredictable and sometimes violent rages. He would scream at me, at drivers who annoyed him, at neighbors who were too loud or who had violated rules known only to him. He had once thrown me against a wall for some perceived threat to his dignity, but mostly his outbursts were verbal. I had absorbed his countless diatribes more times than I could count, or at least cared to count. He once flipped over our dining room table and sent the remnants of our dinner, plates and serving dishes, and silverware crashing to the floor because a television commercial had somehow annoyed him. Living with Fassad was like living with an unstable landmine that could go off with the lightest whisper if something didn't please him.

And Fassad was often displeased.

The odd thing about Fassad was that he had a softer side, an actual alluring and charming side. He was capable of kindness, and in a way I loved him, even after all his ferocious outbursts.

That day I could almost understand his anger. American soldiers were in Iraq and had been for more than a week as Operation Desert Storm rolled on. Fassad was an Iraqi patriot, proud of his country, in love with Saddam Hussein. He was familiar with the Iraqi oil fields now being blown apart on our television screen. As a younger man, he had worked in those same fields before coming to Houston to get his engineering degree.

He loved being in America as well. He had quickly grown to appreciate Houston and school and all America offered. He had reaped many benefits from being over here, but the invasion had unhinged him, and I was once again trying very hard not to be the one to push him over the edge.

Fassad was charming, which, of course, might have been part of the problem with us. He was handsome and could be pleasant if the situation called for it. He could, with little effort, present himself in a way that would attract strangers to him—an especially useful and beguiling talent at that time, when Iraqis were not held in high regard.

When we first met in Houston years before, where flag-waving patriotism and God-bless-America emotions ran higher than in other places in the country, he had somehow managed to avoid problems with his charm, jokes, and machismo. This was Texas, after all, and Texans did not look kindly on people from other states, let alone from different countries.

Fassad had certainly charmed me. I had married him, after all. But that was before his true and erratic and more dangerous side emerged. He had a way of raising his eyebrows in quizzical delight that seemed to say, here is a charming man, so full of life and humor. He was bright and energetic and knew what he wanted from life, and when we married, the future seemed bright.

For me, after all I had been through as a girl and young woman, a chance at love and brightness pulled me to Fassad, blindly. I see that now.

The afternoon he decided to kill himself with my finger on the trigger, he had not slept for days. He sat, chain-smoking Marlboro Lights and running his hands through his hair. He was frantic as we both sat on the comfortable love seat in the den of our Georgia condo. The television had been locked on CNN, and Fassad could not pull himself away as he watched with his arm draped over the couch. His tension grew as missiles dropped into his beloved homeland, and he slowly became unhinged.

My own concern at the time was for the American soldiers, but Fassad would have none of that. It angered him that I did not share his torment.

"Curse you," he said each time I expressed even the slightest bit of sympathy for American soldiers. "These are my people being destroyed by you, the stupid Americans."

He had only days earlier returned from visiting family in Iraq, his patriotic fervor reborn to the point where he began wearing a white *thawb*, the traditional ankle-length Iraqi tunic, wherever he went. It was certainly not a common sight in Georgia at the time. His lunacy seemed to grow as the invasion progressed. Fassad had no qualms about thumbing his nose at Americans.

My sympathy for the young American soldiers was eating away at whatever thin resolve remained. He could not understand that, and as the missiles rained down, his fragile emotions crumbled. Fassad got up from the couch and began to pace.

I should have fled then, of course, as he cursed the Americans and the invasion and smoked his Marlboros. I should have just gotten away from there as fast as I could. But I should have left him much earlier than that. We were incompatible, and yet we stayed together. Ours was a quizzical arrangement to be sure. I made a lot of decisions like that, ones where people would say, stunned, "But how could you? Why did you?"

I'm still trying to figure that out, and over the years, I've begun to understand that in a life where love was always missing, you look for it constantly—even in the wrong places.

That afternoon, I sat frozen in fear, unable to summon even the slightest ounce of common sense that would push me out the door and away from this crazy man so fixated on the television and the invasion of his homeland.

Fassad continued to ramble on about the stupid Americans and the glory of Iraq and Saddam while I sank deeper into the couch. He paced and smoked. The tension was palpable, a fragile filament away from breaking into a full explosion. Fassad often did not need reasons for his explosions. His moods could rise and snap for no reason at all. That day, he actually had a reason, as crazy as it was.

He had dark circles under his eyes from lack of sleep and tight, jittery nerves from too many cigarettes and too much strong coffee.

That afternoon, he decided he would die, just as many of his fellow Iraqis were dying. And for the sins of the American invaders and my sympathy for the young soldiers, he would punish me as well. He reached into a coffee table drawer where he kept a loaded Colt .38 revolver to protect himself against his various real and imagined enemies. When you do business as Fassad did, it was not an unrealistic thing to do.

He pulled the gun from the drawer quickly and leaned into me on the couch. He swept aside the newspaper I had been scanning in an attempt to be invisible. He put the gun in my right hand, then wrapped both of his huge hands around mine and pulled it to his head. Then he pushed me hard against the back of the couch and began forcing my finger onto the trigger. I struggled.

4

"Your fingerprints will be on the trigger when they find my body," he said. "I'll be dead, but you will spend the rest of your life in prison."

In many ways, I had been in a prison most of my life, locked tightly in a world with little light. It had been that way for as long as I could remember. But being locked up for life in an actual penitentiary was not in my plans.

I was powerless as Fassad pressed me back against the couch and slowly moved our hands and the gun to his forehead. I struggled but was unable to push him away or wrest his hands from mine.

The doorbell rang. Fassad froze. Even an instant away from carrying out his impulsive suicide, his overriding instincts to appear as prince charming took control. He could kill himself and bring me down with him, but God forbid he should look bad in front of the neighbors.

He jumped from the couch and answered the door. It was our next-door neighbor, his hands gripping the collar of our Doberman.

"Charlie was loose," he told Fassad, "and I wanted to get him in before he got run over."

I could see Fassad trying to control his rapid breathing, and he reached for the dog's collar.

"Thanks, man. I guess I should fix the lead in the backyard. Appreciate it."

He closed the door and turned to me on the couch, still shaking.

He walked into the kitchen and poured another cup of coffee, his anger somehow dissipated.

I was saved.

I stood from the couch, tentative, drained.

Fassad turned and stared.

"Why are you always like this?" he said, trying to control himself. "Why are you always so tense and nervous? You are like a twitchy woman all the time. It makes me crazy."

I walked to the window and pulled it open, breathing in deeply.

How could I explain that? How could I try to show this stranger who was my husband what I had been through?

First, I thought, I would have to tell him about Saint Louis. And before I could tell him about Saint Louis, I would have to try explain my mother.

TWO

ESCAPING

There were always reactions, and the reactions were never good. No matter how well or how smoothly things were moving along, I startled easily and my heart would race. Sudden noises ignited pure panic and I'd shut down for no apparent reason and tune people out. I found that concentrating on anything useless. I could not lock my mind on anything for more than an instant.

Today, I would be quickly diagnosed with posttraumatic stress disorder. Find a counselor, people would say. Get help. Such things did not exist in the 1970s in Houston, Texas. I was on my own in that respect.

Those startled reactions happened even when things were going well. And when I decided to pack up and move to Houston, things were going well. But it looked to me like there was a light in Houston then, a bit anyway, and I decided to move and let it in.

Soon after I had said good-bye to Jose and headed west, I would be working like crazy, holding down two jobs. I would have two men who wanted to marry me. I would be back in school and enjoying classes despite the frenetic pace of my life. I would have my own apartment and an exciting life in a city that was vibrant and alive.

More than anything, I would be close to the kids, the younger brother and sister I adored—the biggest reason I was able to say good-bye to Jose.

When I got to Houston, I barely had time to breathe because I was so absorbed in it all. Maybe that was what I was trying to do: keep so busy I had no spare time to look back.

But no matter what was going on, no matter how busy I was, the urge to shut down was just a loud noise or an angry comment away.

Houston would prove to be all the things a young woman on her own would want. It offered a chance at love, a chance to make some good money, and a chance to expand horizons. It would take me far from the sordid and violent steps in Seven Hills, away from Alton, away from Sayler Park and Cahokia.

Houston at the beginning had promised to take me away from the madness.

The drawback to it all, the one single thing that anyone would wonder about, was that the move to Houston would bring me back into my mother's orbit—the root of it all, the reason I teetered so close to the edge.

When I first got to Houston, I was on a winning streak, and if I had time to take a breath and suppress the darkness, I might have enjoyed it more than I did. But my mother was hovering in Houston. You'd think that I would have put as much distance as possible between us, as much as I genuinely hated her. My mother had wanted me to surrender my sanity—as most of my siblings had by that time. My mother had predicted I would be an alcoholic, or a drug addict, or a whore. Instead, I grew into a hardworking young woman with suitors and a busy schedule.

Yet somehow I ended up in Houston, living not too far from where she and Ed had settled. Odd, for sure, but that was her dark pull. Ed had tried to leave her, finally, but she convinced him to stay, and they had moved to Houston.

A Mother's Love

In many ways, that time in Houston was all a mirage, a superficial hint that I had not escaped my mother's brutality. In many ways, I could not escape the darkness of my past and certainly not the damage. But I was about to give it my best shot. I was making a strong and determined effort to escape the world my mother had predicted—the world she had actually wanted for me.

After you survive so many attempts to break you down, the only option is to rebuild. I've been rebuilding my whole life. I learned very young that at least trying to rebuild and reinvent and re-create was the only way I would have a life worth living.

Before I picked up and moved to Houston—the day Elvis died, in fact—I had been doing well. I had a terrific job at the Missouri Athletic Club and had moved in with a man I loved—even though he was thirty-one years older and could and often did drink a fifth of scotch in a single day and still function. I loved Jose because he was a kind man. I had not been involved with kindness to any degree most of my life. Kindness was an appealing trait.

I was, of course, jumpy and nervous working at the Missouri Athletic Club. I always was, no matter where I was. I could never at any time single out even a moment of something that resembled calmness. I was unsure how to act in public. A few years in a place like Alton will do that to anyone, I guess.

But I managed, even though my coworkers thought I was odd. I had even attracted the attention of a member of the club, a wealthy lawyer, who asked me out to dinner. I went, hesitantly, despite his handsomeness, worldliness, and easy ways. But the one date scared me. It had been nothing more than a normal date, but it was so odd to me with its normalcy—dinner and conversation—that it scared me. I never went out with the man again.

Jose worked as a waiter at an exclusive restaurant, Al's, in Saint Louis, and I soon moved in with him, despite the age difference and his ability to drain a fifth of J&B almost every day.

A phone call from Houston ended that short reverie with Jose. My sister and brother, Theresa and Steven, were still with my mother, this time living with her and Ed. They sounded so upbeat and made Houston sound like such a paradise that I forgot that hell was just around the corner. Anywhere near my mother and her influence was hell. I know that, had lived there, and yet I still went. Just for a short visit, I told myself.

I was nineteen when I left Jose for what I thought would be a brief and maybe even happy reunion with my brother and sister. I loved those two kids, and when they begged me not to go back to Saint Louis, I could not resist.

I would move to Houston, I decided, despite the fact that my mother was there and despite the fact that I think I loved Jose and his kindness and what had been a happy partnership.

When I told Jose of my decision, he was shaken. He had gone to the airport in Saint Louis to pick me up the day I was supposed to return from my short visit. I was still in Houston. He called later, asking me what had happened.

"I waited all night for you, Betty Boop," he had told me.

"I'm not coming back," I said. I heard him begin to cry.

"I wish you the best," he said.

I still ask myself why I left Jose and why I would go anywhere within a thousand miles of my mother. I don't question why I left Jose and his love and his kindness, necessarily, but I do sometimes wonder why I would go back voluntarily into my mother's dark world.

That was her mysterious attraction. No one could really ever leave my mother. She could always, without much effort, make people forget her violence, her threats, and her ugliness. No one was immune to her pull.

Jose called me later in Houston and begged me to come back. But I never did. My mother knew I wanted her love more than any single thing. She admired herself for sparking that desire in me.

A Mother's Love

She knew I wanted her love, and she enjoyed causing me pain. It was a volatile chemistry she enjoyed. It was a victory for her.

I saw Jose briefly when I returned to Saint Louis to pick up my car and my few belongings. He cried while I packed. But the pull of my mother was too strong.

On the way back to Houston, I heard on the car radio that Elvis had died. Funny how things can lock in a memory. If I hear an Elvis song even today, I am suddenly back in a motel room on the way to Houston and what I had hoped would be a new life.

I was excited about the Houston I had seen on my short visit with the kids. It was flat and gorgeous to me, so different from Saint Louis, Cincinnati, or any of the many places I had been dragged to. It was in the middle of the boom days of the oil business, and there seemed to be money everywhere. In Texas, people were not shy about flashing their money and their apparent success.

Even the hot, muggy weather had a certain appeal.

As I drove to Houston, I thought about the jobs I would get and about finally earning my high school diploma, a tough thing to get when you've spent a few years in a place like Alton.

My mother had always mocked me for wanting an education, and she never hesitated to remind me I was too stupid to graduate from high school. She liked mocking me and telling me I was retarded—a ritual she enjoyed until the day she died.

I went to Houston. And I did have those moments of brightness. I did almost escape my mother. But I was a moth drawn to her flame. Houston would be good. I would have my suitors, my education, and my excitement. I would learn that I was not retarded, that in fact I was bright, adaptable, attractive, and talented.

I would find all that in Houston.

I would also be back in my mother's sphere and its darkness. That was her pull, and that was my problem.

No matter how many steps I took toward the light, she could suck me back to the darkness.

Three

HOUSTON

When my mother was in the room, there was no air left for anyone else to breathe. I knew that. She had been suffocating me for as long as I could remember. She hated me, and I knew that, too. I could go missing for days and she would not care, lamenting only her loss of child-support checks. I would have unspeakable things done to me, and she would tell me it was my fault.

She laughed at me because I had no education.

So why would I willingly pull up my life in Saint Louis, leave a man who loved me and a nice-paying job, to move close to her again?

That is both the undiluted mystery and the everlasting truth about the pull my mother had on me and just about everyone else. It would take me years to learn the hard lesson that looking for love from her was pointless.

I know that now. It was a hard lesson to learn.

But Houston in 1979 did have a lot of good things going for it, and if you remove my mother's darkness from the equation, it was not a bad place to end up as a young woman looking for better things and maybe even a bit of excitement.

A Mother's Love

Houston was booming, and the possibilities were as thick as the wet and humid air. Thoughts of a new life in a new place seemed to make sense. I could leave a lot of debris behind and start again, I thought.

Still shocked by the news of Elvis's passing, I drove nearly non-stop to the Houston suburb of Bellaire, where Ed and my mother had moved after Ed's latest transfer. I would be near my brother and sister—the main reason I had pulled up stakes—and I would simply ignore my mother. Ed was easy to ignore. After years with my mother, he knew how to make himself disappear.

At first, she resorted to her standard, inexplicable, and ugly meanness, insulting me at every chance. She never missed an opportunity to remind me that my plan to get my GED was misinformed, given my lack of intelligence.

"You're retarded," she would say. "There is no point in trying to graduate."

For the most part, I did what I had always done: I ignored her as best as I could.

I wasted no time in Bellaire looking for work and found it the day after I nervously unpacked my bags. I picked up a waitressing job at a Shoney's Big Boy right in town. That would be a temporary solution to my two biggest challenges: getting away from my mother and getting some money.

Within a month, I found better work and an apartment. I moved into Houston and did as much as I could to avoid my mother, to make her disappear. That was fairly easy. I quickly began working seven days a week at three jobs. Hard work always helped me. It kept my mind and my body occupied and prevented me from looking back on where I had been. I never took a single day off. I drove myself hard in Houston. I still do to this day.

In the late 1970s, Houston had earned the nickname Boomtown USA. Around that time, it was not too far removed from being a small backwater city that meant very little to anyone. Even in the early 1960s, Houston was a hick town. Oil changed all that, and when I arrived, I found a certain electricity, with skyscrapers, tony restaurants, and crowds of well-heeled businessmen competing to show who had more money.

The freeways into town were clogged, but no one cared. The price of oil had nearly quadrupled in a matter of years. By the time I moved into my apartment in the city after my short stay with Ed and my mother, there was a certain crazy air to the place. Texans are not shy or introspective, and "If you got it, flaunt it" could easily have been the Houston motto.

The oil boom and its gaudy repercussions also meant new power and status for the countries that made up OPEC, and in Houston large numbers of young Middle Easterners—Iranians, Iraqis, and Saudis—had settled to soak up the charged air, attend universities, and live the good life. Most were in Houston to get engineering degrees and then return home to help pump out the oil and bring in the money.

Shortly after I arrived, the growing trouble in Iran—the ouster of the shah, the Islamic revolution, the hostage situation at the American embassy in Tehran—would put a nasty edge on things for Iranians in Houston, or anywhere else in the country for that matter.

Houston also had, surprisingly in a way, given its deep Southern and conservative values, a fairly vibrant gay community. I worked with many gay men, and they helped me a great deal. It might have been by our common differentness, but I always seemed to bond with gay men.

When I first moved to Bellaire, I knew I would have to get out of my mother's orbit as quickly as I could. And I did.

I found a comfortable efficiency apartment where I lived for almost two years. It had a nice living room–and–kitchen combination that suited me perfectly.

I also quickly fond two jobs, one of which led to a third. The seven-day-a-week schedule suited me just fine. I had no time to think about anything other than work, which was a welcome distraction. I worked to forget, and working in those days in Houston I had little time for reflection. That was good.

During the day, I waitressed at Harrow's, an exclusive upscale restaurant in the city center that drew many wealthy lawyers from the nearby courthouse and big-dealer oil men from the Exxon building down the street. Harrow's was the place to be seen for Houston's growing money elite. My work at the Missouri Athletic Club proved to be good training for both the high-stress work in a busy restaurant and dealing with egos.

I was attractive, young, and efficient. In the alcohol-fueled atmosphere of a Harrow's lunch, that meant much attention. At Harrow's, the diners were always men, and they would drink before lunch, during lunch, and after lunch. A few would ask me out, but I never responded.

I really did nothing for fun. I did not know what fun was. I worked.

At night, I worked at the Nantucket Inn, a seafood buffet that drew hungry crowds. The money was good there, but I would easily bring in more money from tips at Harrow's than what I would for a long night at the Nantucket Inn.

No matter where I was and how submersed I was in the distractions of work, I was never far from the terrors. A sudden crash of dishes in the kitchen, an unexpected jostling between tables, a rude comment—any small thing that most people would brush off— sent me into silent retreat. The worst of these unexpected surprises sometimes made me scream. I could not control the sudden outbursts of panic.

These sudden mood swings did not exactly endear me to my coworkers. I might have been the perfect waitress for the diners, but everyone else found my nervousness and jumpiness hard to take. But the manager, Frank, appreciated that I could handle a room of fifteen tables with ease and efficiency. Many of the waiters were gay men who didn't seem to mind my quirks and tensions. Being openly gay in the macho world of Houston in those days was an act of courage in some ways, and the fact that I might be perceived as weird seemed to appeal to them. I appreciated their kindness.

I tried to return that in other ways. I gave a waitress who often worked the same lunchtime shift some money to get her car fixed. But such was the tension and animosity—jealousy that I was such a good waitress or annoyance that I was so nervous, I am not sure— but she actually resented me for giving her the money.

It was an odd bunch, that crew at Harrow's. The black cooks constantly flirted with me and asked me out. One of my few friends there, the always-eccentric Cindy, was married to a gay man for reasons I never understood. The bartender, Phyllis, a straight-up bitch, tried to make my life as miserable as she could. But nothing could match what I had already been through or even come close. Petty work squabbles were nothing to bother me.

The owners were also impressed with me and attracted by my energy and diligence. It was not long before they discovered I had an aptitude for numbers, and soon enough, I was doing their books, my third job.

I'd begin my day doing the accounting at Harrow's at nine, pick up my lunch shift, work until two or three, change into my Nantucket Inn uniform, and head over there for the packed dinners. It was usually after one before I got home.

The next day, I would do it all again.

The entire time I was grinding out those days, I never stopped thinking about finishing school. I knew I could not attend to my usual draining schedule, take classes, and study. Something had to give, and for me, it was work. I cut back, working only Friday and Saturday nights at Nantucket Inn. They were the busiest anyway, and the money was still good. I still did lunches at Harrow's. The tips were great, and I'd be out by three at the latest on most days. That left me time for school.

I asked a friend, a student at the University of Houston, if she knew someone who could help me, who could tutor and get me ready for the GED exam. She asked around and found someone who said he would be interested. I told my friend to give him my phone number.

His name was Ali, and he was an Iranian philosophy major who had plans to become a college professor. Ali was the kindest man I had ever met.

Our tutoring meetings soon blossomed into a friendship of sorts, but it was a friendship between two naïve children in many ways. I was approaching twenty but had lived such an entirely painful and disrupted life that I was not sure if I even knew how to act. He had lived a sheltered life in Iran and was in many ways unprepared to deal with life in the free-swinging 1970s in the United States. I did not know how to deal with men. He did not know how to deal with women.

Ali was part of a large number of Middle Easterners in Houston at the time, Iranians in particular. They were following the accepted path, courtesy of the growth of OPEC and the growing power of oil: go to the United States, attend a university, avail yourself of Western pleasures and morals, return home, and settle back into the far more conservative Muslim culture. It was a bipolar arrangement for sure.

Ali loved Houston and all its openness and freedom. Yet he took me to anti-American rallies protesting American support of the shah of Iran. He decried American morality while planning to stay here as long as he possibly could. He supported the Iranian Revolution from afar, from the comforts of America. He condemned the American way of life while he immersed himself in it and enjoyed it.

His confusing stances were not that unusual in those days. And the fact of the matter was, when we were alone together, and when he was away from his Iranian friends, he was nice, considerate, kind, and funny. He certainly was not a religious fanatic, I knew, and in many ways he was just posturing, just mouthing the words he did not actually believe. Our friendship deepened.

Bettyrose Woody

Then the trouble began.

All the anti-American posturing by the Iranian students in Houston changed very quickly after the shah was deposed and barely made it out of Iran with his life. Reality set in. The Iranian Revolution was under way, and very soon, students in Tehran had taken over the American embassy, holding the Americans there hostage.

It was not a good time to be an Iranian in the United States. In a place like Houston, where fervent patriotism was as natural as breathing. It was downright dangerous.

Soon, the United States began deporting Iranians. The lines at the airport were long, full of reluctant, sad, and nervous friends I had met who were not looking forward to their new lives back home under Ayatollah Khomeini. There were not too many new discos going up in Tehran at the time.

Ali became very nervous as the tensions escalated. We both distracted ourselves with nightly studying sessions. Ali proved also to be a wonderful, thorough, and patient tutor. He often complimented me on the quickness of my mind and my intelligence. It was certainly nothing I had ever heard from my mother.

But any exhilaration I felt at accomplishing something I had set my heart and mind on soon disappeared. I doubt I was looking for some sort of congratulations from my mother, but I suppose in some vague way I was. I was not surprised when she said nothing after I told her I was a graduate.

My mother did not allow her children to ever do anything she hadn't accomplished herself.

I did not go to the graduation ceremony.

I had expected I would graduate. I had expected my mother would ignore it. I had not expected another consequence of my friendship with Ali.

He asked me to marry him, and he made no effort to hide his motivation. He needed a green card, the immigration jackpot that

18

would allow him to stay in America. Suddenly, the conservative values of Iran he had once so vocally supported at those rallies did not seem as appealing to him. I knew that he was asking me to marry him as a matter of convenience, and he knew I knew that.

I couldn't help but ask the obvious question.

"Do you love me?"

"I don't have to love you now," he said in his sweet and honest way. "That can come later."

That was not what I wanted.

Neither did I want what was about to happen. I just didn't know it yet.

Four

COLLISIONS

I did not see the fire truck rolling through the stop sign that morning and didn't slow down my Ford Pinto as I headed into the intersection. We met just past the corner at twenty miles an hour. The impact was loud, sudden, and devastating. It did not take too much of an impact to damage a Ford Pinto.

The fire truck never slowed, and when it T-boned me, my car's right side buckled as if it were made of aluminum foil, which it might have been. Ford Pintos were not known for their sturdiness or their safety records.

I was lucky to be able to put my shoulder to the driver's side door and force it open. I stepped out unhurt.

The car, of course, was totaled.

Because of that one fairly routine accident, my life would never be the same again. I walked away from the crash scene and into a new kind of craziness I am still trying to figure out.

At the time, my odd friendship with Ali was not meshing. The tensions over the hostage situation at the American embassy in Tehran had made it very difficult for anyone who appeared to be from the Middle East to even walk about Houston. Ali was nervous. He wanted to stay in Houston, finish his degree, and apply for graduate school. The last place he wanted to be was Iran. To him, the solution was simple. Marry me, get a green card, and be home free. The matter of love was inconsequential to him. He could not understand why I wouldn't accept his proposal.

In many ways, he was still very immature and incapable of understanding the complexities of relationships. In Iran, marriages were arranged. If we were living in Iran, it would have been simple. His parents would have approached mine, and it would have been settled if the economics made sense. But of course we weren't.

I began to distance myself from him. Having been through my own trials, I was not exactly the model of stability or maturity myself at that time. Spending most of your childhood in hell will do that to you. I did not trust too many people, and I did not feel comfortable outside of work. I was still trying to figure out where I was and what I wanted to do.

I was thankful to Ali for helping me. That was as far as I wanted to go. I knew I wanted love. Never having truly experienced it at twenty-three years old, I wasn't sure I even knew what it was. I did know what it wasn't. It wasn't anything my mother had ever shown or done.

Wanting love when you don't know what it actually is is not that different from a child saying she wants to walk on the moon. It seems like a wonderful idea, but there is no context. There is no one around to show you.

I began to pull away from Ali. I still liked him, and I still sometimes enjoyed his company. But his nervousness about even walking around the city, and his fear of being deported back to what was being reported every day in the newspapers and on television as an increasingly chaotic situation in Iran, had made him unpredictable.

The more I tried to stay away from him, the more irrational he became. He started following me. He stopped by Harrow's and tried to speak to me, which was impossible when I was in the middle of a busy lunch. He stopped by the Nantucket Inn at night. He had no sense of guile, no idea that his cloying presence made me nervous. He often left flowers on my car and wrote long letters professing his undying love for me.

By then, I had proved I was a survivor, and had shown I was bright and could adapt to just about anything. But I was barely used to life on my own. A few years at Alton will tend to make one a little skittish. A lifetime spent in my mother's shadow had not done wonders for my self-confidence.

Being stalked by a lovelorn Iranian was troublesome, but I did not have the slightest idea of how to confront him and end the situation. I had no idea how to react when he moved into my apartment complex with a friend.

My only solace and advice came from the apartment managers, a pair of sophisticated Mexican women in their sixties with a great sense of humor and worldliness that comforted me. They had taken me under their wings, so to speak. They must have sensed something about this wide-eyed young woman who worked so much and seemed so nervous. They were fun, entertaining, and protective of me. They were worldly enough to tell me to stay away from the crazy Iranian and to keep their eyes on him.

When a friend of Ali's knocked on my apartment door and told me Ali had a gun and would kill himself shortly, I ran to my friends, the managers. They calmed me down and called the police, who responded and disarmed Ali, who I suspect was only looking for a dramatic way to have me run to him.

Ali's next cry for attention was his announcement that he was moving to Brazil. If I would not marry him, he was not about to return to Iran and into the arms of the increasingly militant Islamic students who were running wild under the new Iranian leader, the Ayatollah Khomeini. Brazil would be a safer alternative. This time, I called the police, who told him to leave me alone. That's when the real adventure started.

A Mother's Love

I had run into the fire truck and totaled the Pinto. I had to get to work and needed a car desperately. Houston is not a city designed for pedestrians. It is spread out and laced with major highways. Houston is a city for drivers. Without a car, I was stuck and at the mercy of Ali, who was still threatening to head off to Brazil.

The morning after the accident, I walked next door to my neighbor's apartment and asked to borrow a newspaper so I could scan the classifieds for a new car. I had seen him around the apartment complex but had never spoken to him, just occasionally nodded when we crossed paths. I also saw him in the mornings tossing bundles of the *Houston Chronicle* into the back of his pickup. His name, I knew, was Fassad, but that is all I knew. I did know he seemed industrious. He was always working, and I rarely saw him sitting on his small front porch. That morning he was.

I told him about my car situation and asked to borrow a paper. We began talking. Fassad was an Iraqi and an engineering student at San Jacinto College. He worked as a distributor for the *Chronicle*, among other jobs. He gave me a paper and smiled. Unlike Ali, Fassad was emphatically macho. He was big and muscular and made no effort to hide the fact that he found me attractive. I found him attractive myself, in my own naïve way, and I suppose it showed.

He knocked on my door the next morning and told me he had two pickups and wanted me to use one until I found a car. I thought that was a kind gesture and took him up on his offer and drove his red Toyota pickup to Harrow's that morning to do the books. That gesture and Fassad's new attentiveness was the first spark in a different kind of Middle Eastern conflict. Iranians and Iraqis do not hold one another in high esteem. Fassad's attention did little to improve that situation.

Ali, who had apparently been observing my new closeness with Fassad, went immediately to Fassad's apartment. He ordered

Fassad to stay away from me, to not speak to me, and to take his truck back.

Fassad and Ali were two different types of men. They could easily have been from different planets. Ali was kind and gentle. Fassad was ostentatiously macho and acted like it. He stood out because of it. And standing out in the cowboy world of Houston was no small feat. Yet he did. I honestly think he felt superior to everyone. He drove wildly, speeding, cutting in and out of lanes as fast as he could, and swearing at anyone who dared to honk or gesture at him. Nothing bothered him, and he was not embarrassed by his explosive temper, which he wore like a trophy. He certainly was not afraid to make large and theatrical shows of his affection for me.

While Ali would quietly put flowers on my car or write long and sensitive notes, Fassad basically took me prisoner. There was nothing subtle in his approach to courtship. The day I accepted his offer of the truck, he told me he loved me. "You are gorgeous," he would say. "You are beautiful."

Before Fassad and Ali's battle for me started, the men I had known in Houston were the gay waiters at Harrow's. I was in over my head as the battle intensified. Middle Eastern men, it seemed, were a bit different. They did not play games, and there was nothing subtle in their approaches. Fassad asked me to marry him after one day of talking.

Fassad had known Ali had also proposed and that he wanted a green card, which he found ridiculous, weak, and somehow less than manly. He thought Ali was a coward for being afraid to return to Iran. Fassad was a proud Iraqi and made no effort to hide that fact. Fassad explained he had student visa and did not need a green card. He added that he was afraid of nothing. Fassad loved the United States and the freedom and opportunities he saw in front of him, but he was not afraid of retuning to Iraq if he had to. The Iranian was a weakling, he said. Fassad asked me to marry him again less than a week after we had first started talking. This time, I said yes.

Why I accepted lies buried under the many layers of sediment my life had been collecting to that point. I was twenty-three years old. I had never lived anything close to a normal life. I am still scraping away those layers, hoping at some point I will understand. Oddly, saying yes to Fassad somehow made me feel sympathy for Ali and his predicament. Spending time with Fassad and his bluster, noise, and testosterone made me suddenly appreciate Ali's sensitivity.

The night before I was to marry Fassad, I went to the flower shop where Ali and his friends worked. I'm not sure why. I think I wanted to apologize, though I didn't. I think I wanted to feel his gentleness one more time before I stepped into the storm that was Fassad's life.

Ali had little to say to me. One of Ali's friends, another Iranian I had seen around the apartment complex from time to time named Changas, walked up to me as I tried to explain to Ali what I was doing. Changas had been fiddling with something on a bench in the back of the shop. As he approached, I saw he had made me a headpiece from several stalks of roses.

"Here is your crown, just like Jesus wore," he told me as he gave me the headpiece, thorns and all.

The next day, March 10, 1980, I went to the main Houston courthouse, near Harrow's, with Fassad and a wedding party comprised of my friend Janie and two Saudi friends of Fassad's. We were married by a Justice of the Peace in a quick, unadorned ceremony. Our wedding reception was a two-hour dinner at the Aku Aku Islander, a Polynesian restaurant in suburban Sugar Land.

It hit me when we returned to my apartment that night for another party. I might have married the wrong guy. I wanted to see Ali. Fassad was not pleased by my sudden announcement that I wanted to walk over to Ali's apartment. He told me I was crazy and reminded me I was now married to him.

The next morning after Fassad left for class, I tried to find Ali but could not. I first went to the flower shop, but he was not there, and no one knew where he was. I went to his apartment and knocked on the door. It was unlocked and swung open. No one was there, and the apartment was empty. I walked slowly over to the manager's apartment. They told me Ali had moved. "He is heartbroken and had been talking again of killing himself," they said.

I found Ali at a Denny's down the road, sitting disconsolately at a table with a friend. He looked up when he saw me, stood, and left quickly. I did not have time to explain anything, though I was not sure what I was trying to explain or why I had been searching for him. I'm still not sure myself, almost forty years later.

Later that day, I went to the bar where Ali had been working and found him. This time, he did not try to walk out. He was leaving in a few days, he said, going to Brazil. He had a visa and was at least no longer worried about having to return to the chaos in Iran. The next day, I called the bar to speak, but he was gone.

A week later, Fassad found several boxes on his front step. In them were Ali's stereo equipment, a television, and a gun. Beside the boxes were several chairs and a night table from Ali's apartment. A few days after that, I received a package in the mail containing a mirrored clock adorned with birds, one of Ali's favorite possessions. A note was taped to the mirror. I bent down slowly and pulled it off.

"I will see you in my dreams."

Five

HONEYMOONS

Fassad had no time for honeymoons. I doubt the thought ever occurred to him that we should start our married life together calmly. Fassad had no time for calmness either. He seemed to take energy from chaos, relish it, chew it up, then look for more.

I was not so sure of what to expect about marriage myself. I had never had anything that resembled a honeymoon or calmness in my life at that point. If I had had hopes in that direction, they were based on made-for-TV dramas, not on my life. I had nothing then to look back on and hope that it would return. Nostalgia for the good old days was not part of my life.

I suppose, looking back on our hasty marriage, I did have hopes. I always had hope. But I guess now I did not really think much would change in my life after my impulsive decision to marry Fassad. Even today, I wonder about what would have happened if I had married the kind and sensitive Iranian. There is no sense in trying to change the past, but I think I would have had a gentler path than the rocky journey I took with Fassad.

Fassad, a man without a compass, followed his impulses in the general direction of his chief goal: making money. He did anything that pulled him in that direction. His sense of morality, of right and wrong, was blurred, to say the least. He did what he had to do to make money as fast as he could and by any means. He left a lot of angry people in his wake.

And he brought me along for the ride. He was in love with money, not me. Even though I think he was happy, he had acquired part of what he thought was the American dream, a beautiful blonde wife. He saw me as a trophy, not a partner or anything close to a true wife—or at least the American concept of it.

It was not as if he took the money he had made and lavished me with gifts and a life of luxury. He spent his money as quickly as he brought it in, to my chagrin, on women, partying, and things he did not invite me to share. As I look back on it, I suppose I did not expect things to improve much after our hasty marriage, and they didn't. But it was quite a ride.

Later, we adopted a child and looked like a normal couple. Of course, we weren't. I should have known that from the beginning of our marriage, but I should have known that before I impulsively told him I would marry him. I should have known many things by that time, given what I had been through. But life with Fassad was in a way very much like life with my mother. I simply tried to disappear into myself as much as I could and let it pass me by.

I often think of a lyric in a song by Bob Seger that will play occasionally in the back of my mind when I have the energy to look back on things. It's really a powerful biography in eleven words, and it captures my own life pretty well: "I wish I didn't know now what I didn't know then."

It was a given from the start that Fassad had his own way of doing things, and his own way of doing things did not have room for accommodating the wishes of others, especially me.

"You are married to me now. Not that Iranian," he told me on our first night together. "You are an Iranian lover," he said. That would become his name for me. Given that his native Iraq was at war with Iran, that Iraqis hated Iranians, it was not a good thing.

A Mother's Love

"That son of a bitch Iranian. What a fool," he would say, laughing.

Then he took control of our life. He took my car, leaving me without transportation. Then he told me we were moving, leaving me without my friends. After that, he called my work and told them I quit, leaving me without money. It happened so quickly and fluidly that I did not have time to react. Within a month, I was newly married, without a car, without money, and without friends. I was just where Fassad wanted me to be. I was trapped. I could easily have been living in Iraq, where women were supposed to be submissive, obedient, and out of sight.

Oddly, there was love, though in a muted form. He tried to make our life comfortable, and he tried in his own way to show he loved me, and I think he truly did. Fassad could be gentle and caring when he wanted to be. I know he wanted to make my life comfortable. Fassad was strong, he was handsome, and he was in a way a fairy-tale prince who had swept me off my feet. But it was more like being swept away by a landslide. Considering my life with my mother, he was caring and considerate. He would try on occasion to show his love, but it was always on his terms. After one of our many arguments in those early days, he turned to me, put his hands on my shoulders, and said, "Bitch, I love you."

He just did not get it. Fassad, to be clear, was not a violent man. He never hit me or threatened me. Fassad's way was more of benign neglect, of thinking he was actually helping when his self-absorption never allowed him to look beyond his own interests. If I had to encapsulate my fiery years with Fassad, that soft gesture of near kindness and that backward expression of affection would sum it up.

I knew by then that things in life were not black and white, that there was not a clear, distinct dividing line between good and evil. At the time, I still hoped for some sign of affection from my mother, for one glorious nod or hug that would erase the years of darkness with her. With Fassad, I held that same hope. Hope dies hard.

An engineer by trade, education, and aptitude, Fassad was good with cars. He loved cars. Because he loved money and the potential for fast and lucrative deals that would bring it in quickly, Fassad, I learned soon after our marriage, was involved in a deal that imported Mercedes from Europe to sell in the Houston area. Even though the economy was going flat and would soon collapse, when he started the Mercedes scheme, money and prestige were paramount in Houston's oil-money lifestyle. It was important in the big-oil business to show one's power. Driving a new Mercedes did the trick.

Nothing said money and prestige more loudly than a Mercedes, and at first, the business was booming. Fassad would convert the imports to comply with American emissions standards—or at least say he did—and would then quickly sell the cars, cash only.

Whether he actually had done the work or just forged the documents was a question I never asked. Whether the cars were stolen, which a friend of Fassad's had told me, I never brought up.

I learned very early in our marriage that it was best to not question anything Fassad was involved in.

There was no doubt that when he wanted to be, he was very good at what he did. He had persuaded me to marry him in a very short time, after all. Fassad, with his love of cars and his gift of talk, got a job selling Mitsubishis for a time when the Mercedes operation was ebbing. He quickly became the dealership's top salesman.

That was the thing about Fassad. If he was remotely interested in going by the book, in doing things the way the traditional American success story was supposed to unfold, he would have ended up owning the dealership, maybe even several dealerships. He would have been an inspiration, an Iraqi Horatio Alger, who had by his hard work and high ideals made himself a success. Fassad had no interest in that story, though. He loved intrigue and, I suppose, the excitement that went hand in hand with pulling off illicit deals and getting away with it.

A Mother's Love

When you live in a house of cards, though, at some point it will collapse. As bright as Fassad was, he was too caught up in the high volume of cash the Mercedes scam was pulling in to notice the economy was slowly going downhill. The boom days were over, but he did not pay attention.

Fassad would then make a mistake that would send us quickly from the Houston area that I had grown to love. It was the first mistake, the first misstep I had seen him make. It would not be the last in our tumultuous relationship over the years, but it was substantial. I should have known, and I should have warned him, but my role was to remain silent, and I was good at that.

Fassad invested most of his Mercedes cash into a bar, which he and his partners thought would be a magnetic nightclub, with a Mexican motif. It was a big warehouse of a place. He just knew it would be a godsend to the soldiers from a nearby army base. It would be where everyone could shed the daily drudgery and pretend to be high rollers. They could all be swingers, just like Club 54 in New York, except it was in the Texas hinterland, and the clients were soldiers and not New York celebrities. I suspect Fassad also knew it would be a tremendous place to meet women and to play the role of the grand, glorious, and enormously wealthy club owner. That was his American dream—to be the high-rolling American gangster in the movies he loved to watch.

His plans seemed good on paper.

In reality, despite the high plans and grand dreams, the bar was really nothing more than a low-rent rock-and-roll barn, with cheap beer and cheap women.

He and his partner rented what had been a big and popular grocery store. That should have been his first clue. That a grocery store had been forced to close should have been a warning that the economy was weakening, but it had no effect on Fassad. He and his partner bought used tables and chairs from a failed restaurant for $10,000, which should have been another hint.

Fassad was always so sure of himself that he felt he was immune to such things. They built a dance floor and a stage, installed state-of-the-art turntables, and bought hundreds of recordings. They hired a full-time DJ. To guarantee steady and large crowds, they decided not to charge a cover fee.

It was a recipe for disaster, and the disaster was not long in arriving.

A man of dramatic mood swings, Fassad was on a high, and when he was that way, I did nothing to challenge or change it.

It was not a good combination, lots of unmonitored cash and lots of alcohol, drugs, and compliant women who were looking for both.

Fassad loved it at first, but it was inevitable that the dream would take a huge downfall. Fassad's Mexican bar headed south quickly. I saw very little of him in those days, and I was fine with that. I enjoyed the relief, in fact.

As the weeks of bar ownership began to erode Fassad's confidence and his cash flow, he would come back to our condo, looking exhausted and spent. As agile as Fassad's mind was and as smart as he was, he did not see it coming. I did, by his moods, which became progressively worse. I would learn later that when Fassad was under pressure, his decision making became desperate and clouded by panic. Rather than pull in and circle the wagons, Fassad became rasher in what he did. Most people would look at the hemorrhaging cash and try to stop it, but Fassad only dug himself in deeper.

I do not know what preceded the night Fassad came home and told me to pack. I do not know what he had done to spark that nervousness and urgency. I had learned enough by that time to never ask but to simply obey.

"We have to leave," he told me that night. "We're moving to Georgia."

It did not strike me until much later, but it was Halloween night. It was a perfect time for my life of charades with Fassad to take its next turn.

Six

HAVING A BABY

I wanted a child. More than anything I wanted a beautiful, innocent baby boy I could love. Growing up without a whisper of affection had left me desperate to shower a baby with the love I never had. I did have passing glimpses of love and the energy that flowed from it. I had seen families in my earlier childhood, although far too briefly, show what love meant and what it could be like. It seemed to me so peaceful and reassuring, the way they lived and laughed together. I wanted that. I dreamed of having a baby and adoring him. In return, the baby would love me. It seemed like an ideal arrangement, a full circle of loving and giving.

Of course, there were complications, but I was by then deft at dealing with complications. I was resilient and not at all intimidated by obstacles that had been thrown my way. Although I was shy and not entirely comfortable with being assertive by the time Fassad and I had settled into our version of married life, my desire to have a baby drove me. I was not shy about expressing my feelings or doing all I could to erase the complications. Fassad, in only the odd way that he could be, would prove to be helpful.

I had learned earlier, long before I met and married Fassad, that pelvic inflammatory disease had blocked my fallopian tubes. What had possibly led to that disease was too difficult for me to dwell on at the time and still is, in fact. It did not matter. I was not going to accept the verdict of one doctor based on one examination.

I saw several doctors, asking each time for a different verdict, hoping the previous doctor and previous exam had somehow missed something, had perhaps been careless. Each time, I heard the same thing.

"No. I'm afraid your tubes are blocked. There is nothing I can do. I'm so very sorry."

I kept searching for an answer, though, a miracle doctor who would help me. If you look long enough, you will always find what you want. It is a universal given that people with hopes beyond the realities of the presented facts will always find someone willing to sell it to them. I have a secret cure for cancer. I have a stock tip guaranteed to make you a fortune. I know the secret formula.

If you want something bad enough, you will believe the answer is right around the corner. Hope, realistic or not, will blind people to reality. And when it does, there will always be someone there to give you your dreams. For a price, of course. I continued looking, and I finally found someone willing to sell me my dreams.

"I believe we can fix this," a Houston gynecologist told me. "All you need is a simple procedure. I've done hundreds of them with great success. Your tubes are not permanently blocked. After my procedure, you will be fine and able to have a baby when the time is right. Believe me."

I did believe him. He was not operating out of a back-alley office. He was associated with a major medical center in Houston, his credentials further polished by a professorship. It would turn out later he had a PhD in perfidy and a graduate degree in greed. But he was a master at selling hope. I bought in. He performed the surgery and told me as I woke that it was successful. I was ecstatic.

A Mother's Love

When I married Fassad, the doctor completed the charade by prescribing fertility drugs. He assured me I would soon be pregnant, and I would have the baby I wanted so badly.

But nothing happened. By that time, Fassad and I had moved to Georgia, his nightclub dreams in tatters and his need to leave Houston still unexplained.

We had been trying to conceive, but trying and hopeful expectation had produced nothing. After the procedure and the fertility drugs, I was giddy with joy and impatient for the inevitable. The inevitable never happened, though my doctor kept assuring me it would be only a matter of time.

My impatience trumped hope, though, and I sought another opinion. I was relentless in my search for an answer and in those pre-Internet days made dozens of phone calls and had dozens of appointments.

The path would lead me to Worcester, Massachusetts, where I would learn about the lie. I would know that while hopes die hard, mine were dead and had been dead for years. I just did not know it. The Houston doctor had sold me a lie, and I was so wrapped up in my dreams that I did not see it.

In Worcester, I learned that the Houston doctor had not fixed a thing. He had, in fact, removed one of my fallopian tubes and cut the other so radically that it was useless. I would never have children, the doctors in Massachusetts told me. I was devastated, and I grieved as if I had lost a living child.

I returned to my hotel, stunned and numb, trying to absorb the news. I had been so optimistic and had so readily placed my faith the Houston doctor, the thought that he had been a fraud had never occurred to me.

In the lobby, waiting for the airport shuttle, the horror of it all overtook me, and I became hysterical. I screamed, shook, and lost control, and the emotions I had kept safely covered and in control ran amok. The shocked shuttle driver, entering the lobby to collect my luggage, hurried over to me and wrapped me in her arms. She tried desperately to calm me, to offer some sort of comfort. She walked me gently around the lobby until my nerves calmed, never taking the lit cigarette she had been smoking from her mouth. I can still smell it now—the ashes and smoke like my dreams.

When I returned to Georgia and Fassad, I did what I had always done in crises. I pulled back and tried not to expose myself or put my emotions on display. Once again, they were battered. I would break down at the sight of a couple with a newborn child. I would weep at happy television families. I'd cry for no reason at all. I was overwhelmed and unable to stop thinking about my childless future. I had enjoyed the dream so much and the hope of mother-hood and all it would bring, that the darkness of my life and my mother was for a time blotted out, forgotten.

After Worcester, the darkness started once again to make its presence felt. The childhood memories I locked away began to slowly crawl back in. Fassad became an unwitting ally. He watched me grieve and seeing my hurt bothered him, though being Fassad, it had at first annoyed him. He asked ask me to stop crying, and showed more annoyance than sympathy. Fassad was not an empathetic man, so caught up in himself and his dreams of money.

One afternoon, as he sat across the dining room table from me, I told him, my eyes red and puffed from crying, "No one will love me if I don't have a baby."

That seemed to have struck a nerve.

"My mother would have been devastated if she could not have children," he said.

"Then why can't I grieve like your mother would have?" I asked.

In typical Fassad way, he expressed his feelings. "I love you, bitch."

It was an odd moment of sympathy from a man who hid his emotions so coolly and skillfully. But family meant everything to

Fassad, and the context of his mother and his own family seemed to wake him up to what I must have felt.

I was dumbstruck and bolstered. That single expression of affection from Fassad sent me along a path I had only vaguely thought about. We would adopt. I had a husband who loved me, and together we would adopt a baby.

That single comment burst through every defense I had drawn around myself. It awakened me from my predictable fallback of pulling into myself and not letting anyone or anything reach me. Fassad loved me, understood me, and wanted to help me. He wanted to help us. We would try. I set about doing as much research as possible, as fast as possible.

I knew immediately and without reservation that I would be a wonderful, doting, loving, unflappable mother. That had always been my dream, and now my husband would help me realize that dream. I was close to ecstatic. But then, an intruding thought burst my dreams.

My mother.

If she found out what I was planning, she would find a way to ruin it. She had made my misery one of her chief occupations. A hint that I might bring love into my own life and in turn be loved would make my mother insane. It would be only a matter of time before she would come up with a way to sabotage the plan. It was also most inevitable.

She could not help herself. Once I learned of the Houston doctor's fraud, that he had lied and led me on, I filed a malpractice suit. A futile gesture, I would realize, but it did give me some satisfaction. My mother, who always managed to find a way to invade my life even when I was nowhere near her, had called the doctor and told him I was planning to kill him. That, of course, caused problems and led to the doctor hiring a bodyguard. My mother loved the confusion she had prompted.

Bettyrose Woody

Researching the adoption process in Georgia, thinking about my mother and her long reach, I convinced myself she would find a way to ruin it. At some point, social services would do the requisite research, investigating my past and Fassad's, interviewing employers and neighbors, and visiting our home and speaking with us.

Then at some point, I knew they would want to speak to family members about my suitability as a mother. That was when my mother would strike, and that was when the adoption process would come to an abrupt halt. I knew it.

It was pure serendipity, but one night while Fassad was out on one of his habitual long walks, I watched a segment on the television show *20/20* on a recent trend in adopting babies from Romania, where political upheavals had lifted the secrecy of that Balkan nation. The doors were opening in Romania, and many babies were available for adoption. We would adopt a Romanian baby, I knew.

When Fassad returned home from his walk, I told him what I had decided. He took no time in agreeing, and we set to work the next day with a call to the Georgia Department of Social Services, which had to approve any adoption. We scheduled the first of what would be several interviews for the next day.

My fear that my mother would intrude and ruin my dream had become so real I barely slept, various scenarios of how my mother would insert her wickedness turning over in my head. The social worker was a petite middle-aged woman who walked through the condo and, I suppose, somehow intuited how we lived and how we would care for a child. As she prepared to leave, she stopped and smiled as she gathered her notebooks and the various papers she had had us fill out and sign.

"I'll need references, of course," she said.

My heart sank.

She continued.

A Mother's Love

"For obvious reasons, we cannot accept references from family members. We feel they would not be fair and obviously not impartial. We have found that family references are not useful."

My mother would be barred from interfering. I breathed an immense sigh of relief.

Next, we set about planning, and Fassad's single-mindedness helped immensely. We found an agency that would help us get in touch with an orphanage in Bucharest. That led to more interviews and more background checks seeking to learn if we were emotionally and financially capable of adopting and caring for a child. Without my mother, we passed. The biggest hurdle was cleared.

Next, Fassad went to the Romanian consulate in Atlanta and got a visa for his travels. We had discussed the importance of finding a baby boy. That was my only stipulation. The rest would be up to Fassad. I did not want a girl. My mother would have hated a girl—as she hated me. I was not going to give her the opportunity to crush a new generation of children.

Fassad understood, but being Fassad, he took his own path once he got to Romania. He did everything on his own, and as it turned out, a one-week trip there extended itself to more than a month. He did not like the chaotic and depressing orphanages and their available babies. He hired a lawyer in Bucharest and began his own search for a child who had not been exposed to the cruel life of Romanian orphanages.

With the attorney's help, he found a beautiful thirteen-month-old baby boy, born on April 6, 1990, whose mother was a Gypsy, a Roma, as they were called. The boy was her eighth child, and she simply could not care for him.

Fassad did everything on his own while I sat back in Georgia. I knew nothing of what he had done or how he had done it until I got a phone call from Romania, where he was holding our new son on Sunday night. I loved the sound of that, *our son.*

"I will be landing back at Hartsfield Monday night at eleven, Delta one-ten from New York," he told me.

I spent the next day on a cloud, beyond happy.

Monday night, I made the hour-long drive to Hartsfield Atlanta airport, parked, and went directly to the Delta gate where I waited. I saw no sign of Fassad or our new son. I sat and watched as passengers pulled their luggage from the flight carousel until it stopped, empty.

There was still no sign of Fassad.

I had no idea while I sat there the always-impatient Fassad had not seen me and had taken a taxi home. Our new son had soiled his diapers, and Fassad had decided that the best course of action was to leave. I would find them later, he reasoned. With no cell phones, he could not call.

When I called home, Fassad was already there and explained the situation. I did not care, nor was I angry, nor did I complain. My dream had arrived and was at home. That was all I needed to hear. I don't remember the drive home.

I remember only walking in the door and seeing Fassad fast asleep on the couch, still cradling in one arm a bottle. In his other arm, fast asleep, was our new son, whom we would name Allen. It was the most beautiful scene I had ever witnessed. I picked up Allen from Fassad's arms and kissed him gently.

Seven

KENTUCKY

As she saw herself, my mother was the producer, writer, direc-tor, and star of a movie in which she was the central and only focus. It was a movie she saw every day of her life, a film in which she graced others with her kindness and untold sacrifices. In her own mind at least, she was a heroic and gentle figure, a woman everyone loved. The reality was far different.

My mother loved the Bethany Christian Mission Center, and she loved Miss Marjorie Burt. Maybe that's what is most telling about her, loving a Depression-era orphanage and all its severity and hardness. My mother did not love too many things, certainly not me.

She tried for years to take my sanity, to make me somehow crack and fold into a mindless child. She never explained her hatred for me and never tried to. She did not acknowledge her actions or ever apologize for them. I've tried for years to understand why, to somehow explain how a mother could carry such deep hatred for her own child. Almost sixty years later, with an adoring son and grandchild I would do anything for, I have an idea. But it took distance, time, and a lot of pain to figure it out.

Bettyrose Woody

In my mother's imaginary world, she was a hero, selflessly raising her children in spite of enormous obstacles. She was clever, or maybe devious enough, to convince streams of neighbors, teachers, and social workers this was the case. She could charm, lie, and alter circumstances with little effort. She could attract men who would do anything for her. She could avoid confrontation with a smile and a story. In her own mind, Juanita Greer was a saint.

Juanita Greer, known to everyone as Jackie, was born in Paris, Kentucky, a hard-edged Appalachian town in 1929, the year the stock market crashed and America began its long struggle back to economic recovery. People across the country suffered much during the Great Depression, but people in Appalachia suffered more.

No doubt my mother had it hard—very hard. She and her family lived in dire poverty in the starkest of places in the darkest of times. Eastern Kentucky was hit hard by the Great Depression, and to make things tougher, to really top it off, her father was a drunk and abusive man with little or no time for his children. Her mother, my grandmother, was by all family accounts a kindhearted, if struggling, woman who did everything she could to find food and shelter for her children. She was overwhelmed but never stopped trying. She did what she had to do to get by. How she did so I will never know. And she made great sacrifices, including giving up her children to the Bethany Christian Mission Center.

According to an account of her life written many years later by my mother, my grandmother pulled everyone through. But like many things my mother did, we're not sure how much of her retelling of the family story is true and how much is fiction to make her life and her own suffering stand out. My mother was an artist who could make herself look saintly and perfect, and she was able to fool people her entire life.

But what she failed to do was to show her own children any slight peck of goodness, love, or sympathy. That was reserved for outsiders. Our lives were much different. My mother was incapable of love, and I searched my entire life for it, to understand what it felt like. My mother scarred me for life, and she didn't care. I'm still not certain if she punished me for her own hard times or if she was simply born that way. She was capable of the worst type of hatred—that of a mother for her own children—and for me, she reserved an all-consuming hate.

My mother was gorgeous, and she used her looks and charm to attract people, men especially, her entire life. Her long-suffering mother was a full-blooded Shawnee. Her father, an expert mechanic when he wasn't drinking, a rarity, was never home. He often slept off his drunkenness in the back of the garage he ran in Paris, Kentucky. People in Eastern Kentucky had it hard in those days, but Native Americans had reserved for them an even lower station in that hardscrabble life. My mother got a taste of that life at the bottom.

My grandmother, Louise, married James Greer, who had already had two children from a previous marriage in the late 1920s. Together they had more children, including my mother, their first, born in 1929. Following her in quick succession came Bobby, then Jimmy, and finally Betty Lou, for whom I am named. My mother hated Betty Lou. Perhaps it's an indication of the darkness that drove her that she named me for the sister she despised.

James Greer loved drinking more than anything else, a story as old drinking itself. My grandmother struggled as James's appearances became less frequent. His family was starving, but he cared little. My grandmother struggled, working as a domestic when she could. Times were tough in the isolated mountains.

Before the railroad came through in 1912, there was no way to get to Paris, Kentucky, but walking. And while the railroad brought some spark of boom times, it was short lived. By the time my mother was born, hard times were everywhere. Even as late as the 1990s, Bill Clinton used Harland County as an example of what poverty meant as he promoted national economic programs to help the poor.

A legal document passed down in my family tells my grandmother's story in clear and unemotional terms. And it introduces what would be formative years for the young Greer children as they headed to Bethany. My mother's siblings, Bobby, Jimmy, and Betty Lou, hated those years at Bethany, hated everything about life there. For years, Jimmy would talk about being tied to a bed after he wet it in his sleep. My mother, on the other hand, loved it, or at least professed to love it. That says a lot about the strange mind and emotional state of Jackie Greer. Maybe it says even more about how things would turn out for me as a young girl.

Dated April 1936, a form from the courts lays it out:

"This matter coming on to be heard, upon due and regular proceedings under chapter 18, Article V of the Kentucky Statues (Carroll's Edition. 1915 and 1922).

"All the necessary parties being before the court, all facts and evidence having been heard and considered by the Court, and the Court being advised, it is ordered and adjudged as follows:

"That the neglected and dependent infant named Jackie Greer, of female sex and 6 years of age, indicated in the caption to this order of commitment, be and the same is hereby committed to the Bethany orphanage, there to remain until further ordered by this court."

The form went on to include Jackie's younger siblings as well.

A form detailing a medical examination showed that my mother was "physically and mentally sound" and was not, among other things "deformed," did not have "the itches, measles, mumps, whooping cough, scarlet fever, or chicken pox."

I often think of how my grandmother must have suffered through those years. I have a stack of correspondence—of her loving and hopeful letters to the children, petitions to the court, and pleas to orphanage officials to let the children visit. It's more than two inches thick, testimony to her earnest and heart-wrenching attempts to keep her children safe and fed and maybe even feeling secure as she bounced from menial factory job to cleaning rooms in big-city Cincinnati, probably the only place where work of any kind was available in those lean years.

The Bethany Mission Christian Center on Mission Creek, which still operates today, was founded by Miss Marjorie Burt in 1926 to "Serve Christ in Eastern Kentucky." The home still calls attention to the fact that through its work and its caring for generations of children, "many people have heard the life-changing message of Jesus Christ. What a wonderful testimony to His constant faith and abiding love."

As far as I know, Christ preached compassion and love. Somewhere during the years my mother stayed at the home, she missed the message.

When the Greer children arrived in 1936, the mission had just celebrated its tenth anniversary and had by then cared for some three hundred "orphans"—thirty-one of whom graduated grade school, a rare thing in those days in that part of the country.

My mother, in her lifelong charade, had a soft spot for children who weren't hers. Whether it was from her days at Bethany, I'm not sure. Even on days when she would scream and curse at me for being alive, she'd see a youngster on a playground or in church and would make a big and noticeable fuss.

"You're so cute," she'd say for all to hear. "You're adorable."

At home with her own kids, she sang a different tune, a vicious, hateful tune.

"Jackie was the meanest person I ever knew," said her sister, Betty Lou, now in her eighties. Her brother Jimmy won't speak of her at all.

My mother's account, fiction or not, tells the story.

"There was poverty attached to having a father that drank, even though my father was a high-ranking mechanic in the town and owned the only garage there. He did not support us nor care if we ate or not. The welfare and neighbors seemed to be our main support when my proud mother was not washing, ironing, or sewing at the local overall factory to support us."

There is no doubt things were bleak.

"We took ties to the Christmas show and traded them as admittance fee," she wrote. "I don't think things were ever more fun than at those times, but the last of those trips is fuzzy in my memory."

Tragedy trailed the family. Walking back from one of the Christmas shows my mother so much enjoyed, "One of my sisters became so dizzy that she couldn't stand on her feet. At first we all thought she was teasing, since previously they had been holding me up between them and I was holding my feet way off the ground, which seems to be an amusing game for us alike. At any rate Kate proved she wasn't faking and they helped her home where my mother immediately became concerned and sent for my father.

"He arrived sometime that night late, but before his arrival Kate went into a coma and then out and into some sort of nightmares. She chilled and then would burn up, would call for us to get all the shoes in the house and put them in bed with us, which we did. And then she seemed to become some better and asked my mother to put my baby brother in with her. Jim was the third child so far of my mother's and father's and had been picked by Kate as 'her baby.' She always slept with him and now she fell into a sound sleep.

"During the night she awakened screaming and I watched from the doorway as my whole family tried to convince my father that she should have a doctor and how violently my father resisted them all.

"The next day she was much worse and while daddy was at work my mother took it on herself to call the doctor, who after a brief examination pronounced she had spinal meningitis. An ambulance raced her to the hospital where they gave her spinal taps and she lay in a coma for several weeks. Then she awakened one day seemingly weak but alive, I heard the conversations of my family who had visited her at the time. They couldn't understand why she didn't seem to understand what they were saying but then the realization came to the doctors that this terrible disease had robbed her of her hearing."

My mother was only three at the time, but the memory of her older sister's sickness burned itself into her consciousness. Was it these harsh and unforgiving moments that created the monster? I've tried over the years to understand, to somehow find a reason for the way she treated me. Maybe it was that; maybe the many other trials she endured as a young child. Maybe it was none of these things. Maybe it was just her.

While her mother worked, my mother became a caretaker for her younger siblings. But the fragile existence continued.

She wrote:

"My mother had come home into a dark kitchen and fell over a wash tub which scratched her on the shin. She developed blood poisoning and the doctors were to remove her leg immediately. She didn't have anyone to watch us and by this time our daddy seldom came home unless he was so drunk and abusive, if I can remember it.

"I was to watch and care for three babies [Bobby, Jimmy, and Betty Lou] while she went to the hospital and the awareness that she was sick suddenly came over me, leaving me scared and crying."

But there was mysticism and spirituality up in those hills to go along with the poverty. People who faced dying in the most banal of circumstances, like a scratched shin, often searched for answer from God.

"Miraculously there appeared an old man with a long beard walking up the hill to our porch. I thought him to be a doctor or someone to take mother away like they had taken Kate to the hospital. He carried a black book which turned out to be a Bible and after salutations he asked about my mother's health. Showing him the leg, she told him they were supposed to remove it right away. He was, of course, very sympathetic and after prayer and advice he left. But whether it was his advice, the answer to prayer, or my mother's faith I will never know, but she did take the Baptist preacher's advice and we obtained a can of axle grease and applied it to her shin. The next day the redness was gone and within a week she was up and around again."

My mother wrote that in those days, she was often afraid. It makes sense because her family was forced to move frequently, rely on the kindness of strangers, and were constantly hungry. At times, to ward off the winter-mountain chills, they would go to the entrance of the local mine and scavenge for bits of coal to burn to keep warm. These are the types of things that in most people would create empathy for others. People who have been through tough times rarely forget and often go out of their way to help others who might be in the same situation—who might share a common bond of living through hard and often hopeless times. Empathy was never a strong suit of my mother's. I doubt very much she ever experienced a flash of it.

Was this what drove her? Was this what prompted her unbridled hatred for me?

"Fear was my companion continuously during those years. Fear of daddy, fear of ghosts, fear of the fire place catching the house on fire, fear of the neighbors. Fear of this and that and everything. My mother was young and how frightened she must have been. Since she had no one else to talk to I was her confidante. The same fear followed me through life and remains with me constantly. Though I try to fight, it sometimes overcomes me. I am afraid to walk into a room in the dark. Hearing noises and seeing shadows."

Eventually and inevitably, things became far too much for my grandmother to cope with. The courts intervened, and she was forced to give her young children up because they were so often alone.

A Mother's Love

Under court order, my grandmother still tried to do the best she could. She had heard from a friend about Bethany and set off to see if it was sufficient to care for her children. She had heard that unlike other orphanages, Bethany would not put her children up for adoption. She was willing to do anything for them if they could find safety, warmth, and adequate food, but she was not willing to lose them.

My mother tells of the occasion.

"So leaving us children with a colored family up the creek, my mother took a bus to the home. She was gone a couple of days and returned with new dresses and clothes for us to wear. There were no shoes and the need for them was great with me."

Satisfied that Bethany was the best place, my grandmother packed up the kids and set back out for the hill and Bethany.

My mother wrote:

"With shopping bags crammed and bundles tied, we headed down to the little bus station to make the long trip to Eastern Kentucky. The people on the bus were kind and without their help, no telling what we would have eaten that day.

"Of a sudden the bus driver was helping us and on our feet late that night and he deposited us in the loneliest looking spot I've yet to see. Dogs howled and you couldn't see your hand in front of you. Mother knew the road having just made the trip the previous week. So with her carrying my baby sister and several packages and me half-carrying my little two-year-old brother and half-dragging him we set out. What a little trouper my other brother was. He was only three or four-years-old and he never whimpered but carried a loaded shopping bag that never missed one of the dozens of mud holes we passed on the trip.

"I would put little Jim down and have him walk some but about halfway there he came out with a line that nearly doubled my mother and I up with laughter. 'Ma, my little legs won't carry me no farther,' whereupon my mother stopped by the side of the road. Then she took Jim to carry and I took the baby, Betty."

Bethany became the Greer children's home for the next six years. I doubt there was a single day my grandmother did not despair of the horrible choice she had to make. One of her letters to the children shortly after they had settled in captures her struggle and inner torment. In October 1936, she wrote:

Dearest ones at Bethany,

I am writing after so long. I have been so busy I could not write very well. I have been looking for a job. I could not do all of the work at [College Hill] so I am out of work right now but I will find something to do. I am asking God to help me. I am staying with some good people I knew when I was a girl back home. They are very nice to me but I sleep on the floor for they don't have a bedroom and very little to eat but it keeps me from starving so I am very thankful for it. I feel like that brighter days are ahead for me. I pray every night.

I was so glad for that letter you sent me with that little verse on it and the picture of the children at Bethany. I have been once at God's Little School.

By the early 1940s, the Greer children were still at Bethany, and my grandmother was still signing agreements to keep them there until "each of the said children have reached the age of eighteen or until they have completed the eighth grade of Bethany School."

She never gave up hope.

The children became accustomed to the hardness of life at Bethany and perhaps to feelings that their mother had abandoned them. On her first night at Bethany, my mother wrote of a nightmare she had that sent her flying from her bed and breaking a gas lamp by the bedside. She felt the whole family would be sent away because of it.

"However, they were sympathetic and made lightly of the lamp," she wrote.

That was my mother's introduction to the kindness at Bethany. But that first morning, she also saw something that she carried with her the rest of her life: her mother on the back of a farm-hand's horse, leaving without a good-bye, a disappearance of great pain. It was a wrenching scene to be sure.

She wrote how she felt.

"It was months before we next saw her and during that period I learned to hate her for not showing up around the bend when I wished for it. I learned to live every day waiting and hoping with mixed emotions but at the end of the day I always ended up with the self-abused feelings of hate and love entangled.

"Somewhere along the way my mother and I had also lost something very precious never to recapture it again. The closeness and blind adoring love just wasn't in me any longer. I could see how desperately my mother fought to gain it, and the harder she tried the more I withdrew from her. Never letting her kiss me or pamper me. Never wanting her praise."

Hate became my mother's overriding emotion, one she fed daily, whether it was for her children or one of her husbands.

Love and its warmth and comfort were somehow lost on that road to Bethany, and it would never return to Jackie Greer again for the rest of her life.

Eight

Memories are meant to warm you, to bring comfort and knowing smiles. Mine tear me apart.

By the time I was three-years-old, I had built a protective shell around myself to shut life out. I was a zombie, and I conditioned myself to never express emotion or react to anything, good or bad. I didn't smile, but I didn't cry either. I retreated into that closed world for protection and stayed there for years. Zombies don't have to register what's happening around them or to them—or to even think about it. They just plod ahead, one numb step at a time.

That was more than fifty years ago. Until recently, I kept my childhood memories where they needed to be, buried, tightly locked, and unreachable. Even now, I wonder if it was a mistake to send myself back to those days. Maybe those memories should have stayed where they had been. But it is too late now.

Now that I've forced myself to think about those days, to wake up after so many dead years, the memories storm back, nasty and coming from all directions. I've opened the door, and I can't close it now. I can't keep the memories out. They're like rude and uninvited guests. I think of one thing, and five others rush in to join it. Some memories blend, and the dates and the reasons for them blur.

But others are as clear as the hands in front of my face as I write this.

I remember Spruce Cottage. I can see the placid-looking building now, set back in the trees. It looked like the kind of place that offered serenity and rest and recuperation. Even its name suggested something closer to an inviting summer camp for girls. The name and the neat and ordered exterior of Spruce Cottage was a mirage, though. Spruce Cottage was a madhouse from hell.

I arrived at Spruce Cottage as a twelve-year-old girl who had already seen far more than I should have, all under the guidance and direction of my mother. Why I was there, escorted by police under a court order requested by my mother, had never really registered with me. I just knew I was there and didn't in any way want to be there. In those days, there were many places I would choose not to be if it were up to me. I certainly would not have chosen to be anywhere near my mother.

That was before I stepped inside Spruce Cottage. Once I took my first escorted step through that large black screen door, I knew I was looking into hell.

Spruce Cottage was part of the Alton State Mental Hospital in Alton, Illinois, a small hard-edged town in the south-central part of the state, a bit north of and across the Mississippi from Saint Louis. Then, in the early 1960s, Alton State Mental Hospital was only slightly removed from a time when these horrid places were called asylums and were nothing more than warehouses for the unwanted and uncontrollable—the looney bins, nut houses, and funny farms where crazy people were kept out of sight—often permanently.

I would live at Alton State Mental Hospital for two years, though "live" is a charitable word that might indicate some form of daily existence that was normal and ordered. For me, it was a pure, uninterrupted nightmare, a horrid time made vaguely palatable by the steady regimen of antipsychotic drugs I was forced to ingest each day. I imagine even hell would seem less evil in a long and steady Thorazine fog.

At twelve, I was a small, blond-haired waif of a girl. I doubt I weighed a hundred pounds. By the time I stepped into Spruce Cottage, I had run away from home a number of times. I had spent some time with my father, friends, and relatives of friends. Any place was better than being with my mother and Ed, the man she had told the nuns in Cahokia, Illinois, was her brother. The nuns would not have accepted my mother and her pretend world if they had known otherwise.

At one point, when we were living in Cahokia, my mother had asked one of the nuns if she agreed I was retarded. "No," the nun had replied. I was not retarded, nor was I a problem.

I was a problem only in my mother's eyes.

My mother was always trying to convince neighbors, teachers, social workers, and courtroom figures I was a deeply troubled girl who was prone to violent outbursts, as if a ninety-pound girl could be a threat to anyone.

By the time I stepped into Spruce Cottage, I had already at eleven and twelve been immersed in trouble usually reserved for older girls. All I knew was that everyone, my mother, father, Ed, and many others, were all angry with me, though honestly I had done nothing but be in several wrong places at several wrong times. My mother—always convincing—had told various social workers and court officials I was violent, incorrigible, and uncontrollable and obviously a runaway.

That was a special touch my mother had—pulling herself to the center of her imagined spotlight and offering herself as an example of a long-suffering victim of tragic circumstance.

I needed help, she said. She could do no more for me, try as she might, she said. And because one of my more recent runs was with a group of boys who had picked me up hitchhiking and taken me to Peoria, and because the courts and my mother were in Illinois, Alton was the place for me to finally get help.

My mother was not a stranger to sending loved ones to mental hospitals. She once had my father committed to Longview Hospital in Cincinnati. Perhaps she felt Alton would offer me the haven that Longview did to my father. I had visited him there. It was clean, neat, and quiet. Perhaps my mother felt Alton would offer me some comfort, though my comfort was never a high priority for her. She enjoyed my discomfort and tried as often as she could to make me as uncomfortable as possible.

Alton was not Longview. There were no screaming, drooling people at Longview. There was no violence or urine-soaked hallways.

Alton was not far removed from days when people were termed "acutely excited," "chronic quiet," "chronically disturbed," and "convalescing," then locked away in wards like so much unwanted furniture. By the time I entered Alton, antipsychotic drugs had replaced wet blankets, straightjackets, and lobotomies as a way of control. A few pills and there was no need to do anything but sit back and let the patients drift into their own small worlds, stupefied and unable to do much of anything. I'd learn about that.

In the 1960s, it was possible to place people with slight disabilities in places like Alton, where with the right amount of drugs, they would not bother anyone. I would learn fairly quickly that I was not the only Alton resident who didn't belong there. Not everyone was schizophrenic, disconnected, or chronically depressed. If someone with the right connections wanted to place a troubled soul in a hell like Alton, they could do it with little effort. It really didn't take my mother a lot of work to get me there. I was incorrigible and a runaway, and that was all she needed.

From the outside, the neatly arranged buildings of the Alton State Mental Hospital seemed almost inviting, like the wooded campus of small and friendly college where students walked to classes on tree-lined paths. The appearance of tranquility was emphasized by the names of what they called the "cottages." They bore names like Spruce, Elm, and Pine, as if names could somehow mask what lay behind the doors.

Alton State Mental Hospital was chaos and disquiet and as unsettling as anything in life could be. It was the very model of mental health care in the early 1960s, a warehouse for the raging and unbalanced who could not afford more gracious institutions.

By the time I first stepped into Spruce, I had at twelve-years-old lived in a number of places as my mother continued to reinvent herself. By then, she had left my father and moved in with Ed, taking us along with her. My long-suffering father had himself been sent to Longview at my mother's insistence. My mother left a lot of that in her wake, crazy broken people trying to make sense of living with Jackie Greer. Jackie Greer was an uncontrolled hurricane, and she left a lot of debris in her wake.

Ed coped by withdrawing into himself and letting Jackie control everything, including her four children. My father was a kind man, but he was overwhelmed. The children, especially my old brothers and I, would from time to time escape Mother and live with him. But I never stayed too long.

I had bounced around a lot by then myself, and I'd seen things no child should have seen. No matter where I lived, with my father, with friends, with relatives of friends, I always seemed to end up back with my mother. Before my mother finally convinced the courts I was crazy, she had always told me I was. She'd done that for years.

"I'm sad," I'd tell her.

"Sad?" she'd reply. "You don't know what sad is, you little son of a bitch."

She would illustrate her point by grabbing a handful of my hair near the nape of my neck, twisting it for a good grip around her fist, then shaking my head, whipping it from side to side.

"How's that for sad?" she asked in mock concern.

Few people ever got close enough to see the darkness around Jackie Greer.

With six children—Danny, Grover, Janie, me, Jenny, and the baby, Van—there were almost constant demands on her acting ability, a lot of people she had to convince. Years later, when I emerged from my self-imposed emotional shutdown, I found a used copy of the *Diagnostic and Statistical Manual of Mental Disorders* at a yard sale. It opened my eyes to Jackie Greer and to a topic I'd study later in great detail. This was much later, a long time after she introduced me to Alton, but the words *abnormal love of self, an exaggerated sense of superiority and importance, and a preoccupation with success and power* would make sense.

Her powers of persuasion were remarkable, and I certainly had been running away enough for her to make her point to the courts that I needed, in her words, "proper treatment in a mental institution." Back in those days, when children ran way, it was their fault, never a parent's.

Even today when I catch of whiff of cigar smoke, I think of that long drive. One of the sheriffs who escorted me to Alton, a huge black man, chewed on a cigar for the entire trip. I was frightened beyond belief, paralyzed at what was waiting. I was justified in those fears, believe me.

We met a guard at the main gate leading into Alton, and he took me to Spruce Cottage. The campus looked neat and clean, but appearances are deceiving. Once I stepped through the huge screen door, my new life and all that lay ahead hit me quickly and hard.

The smell was the first thing to overcome me. Spruce Cottage reeked powerfully of urine and catatonic patients sitting in their own feces, untouched for days by anyone. You never get used to something like that. It sinks in and stays.

The air inside never seemed to move, just like the people there. The closed windows and lack of any sort of breeze passing through trapped the desolation, I guess. The residents were disconnected, from one another and from the outside world, drugged into stupors very little could penetrate. Maybe that wasn't such a bad thing.

Life there had a numbing pattern that led nowhere but to the next numb and hopeless day. There was no feeling of any sort of unifying "we're all in this together." There was no feeling at all. Everything moved in slow motion to nowhere.

Before I had reached the door into Spruce, my police escort had taken me to Alton's main office, where I was met by a tall thin man, a security guard whose name I never learned. He took my hand gently and introduced me to a woman dressed in the starched white cleanliness the staff always wore. She hugged me and said hello, a small gesture that I can still feel even today. She knew what awaited me, as did the security guard. Their kindness was something I would treasure over the next two years. Many members of staff were kind, in fact. But they were also powerless to offer much beyond an occasional word of comfort or a pat on the back.

They knew.

The security guard continued to hold my hand as we walked across the wide main expanse of well-maintained lawn to Spruce. He smiled a comforting smile and talked about his children, one a daughter who was around my age, he said. It must have jarred him to know where he was taking me. But his kind words were all he could offer.

I stood paralyzed on the threshold of Spruce, petrified by my first glimpse of the madness inside. The security guard escorted me inside and gently walked me into what would be my home for the next two years. In what he maybe thought was a gesture that would make me more comfortable, he handed me the paper bag my mother had given the sheriffs. Inside was my mother's final joke: dozens of walnuts I would never open.

A Mother's Love

The term *cottage* belies the size of the place. It was neither small nor comfortable. The single-story building housed about one hundred patients—inmates really, because we were all inmates in the craziness. It was primitive and ugly, an unimaginable scene. Some of the people wandering the halls were naked, their hair matted and uncombed. Many were having conversations with unseen companions, a babble understood by no one. Others I saw in the large and open dayroom sat silently, tied to chairs in their own waste. Some screamed occasionally, prompted by unseen demons.

No one seemed to care, neither the other patients nor the staff.

It was like nothing I had ever seen. On the drive, sitting in the back of the police cruiser, I had maintained some small hope that Alton might be something like Longview, where I had visited my father. Longview was at least clean, and it was quiet, and the staff there seemed deferential to the patients. That hope died quickly.

I had been chewing a stick of Wrigley's spearmint gum one of my police escorts had given me on the long ride. As we walked down the main entrance hallway, we passed a small room used by the staff for short breaks and coffee, and I spotted a sink. I reached into my mouth and tossed my gum into the sink. My movement was not unnoticed. I watched, astonished, as a short woman who had been sitting in a chair in the hallway stood quickly, dashed to the sink, picked up my wad of gum, and put it in her mouth.

I would learn later that was Josephine. I would see later her teeth were brown and rotten. Josephine, like most of the patients in Spruce, frightened me.

As I took my first nervous steps down the main hall, deeper inside the bowels of that lunatic place, passersby reached out to touch my blond hair, as if I were a visiting angel. But there were no angels in that place.

Today, I think of my mother's first days at Bethany and her reactions—how she had been paralyzed with fear and anger over her mother's desertion. What drove her to wish the same thing for me, to take such pains to experience the same hell?

My arrival attracted a lot of attention from the people who had enough acquaintance with reality to know a new guest had arrived. One was Vicky, a sixteen-year-old who quickly befriended me, who told me she wasn't crazy either, that she, too, had been forced into this existence.

Vicki was some vague comfort, at least—a sign perhaps that I was not alone. Vicki and I would form an uneasy alliance that would later lead to problems, but she would provide me with an awkward hope that I was not alone.

But others were living in their own worlds. I would become accustomed to an older woman who sat and crocheted without interruption one doily after another, steady and unspeaking. They were beautiful.

In quick order, I also met others shuffling through the halls. Drugs will make you do that, shuffle, mumble, and struggle for clarity. I'd learn that soon enough. One woman chain-smoked as she slowly made her way around. When she finished a cigarette, she would find a nearby chair, sit, and stuff the butt quickly up her nose. Then she would stand and light another cigarette.

Some of the patients were fragile, their only crime being homelessness, or aloneness, lost in a government system whose only answer was to lock them away.

Others were neither fragile, nor innocent, nor wrongly locked up. I would soon meet a small, gnarly, and unshaven man named Bob who smoked Chesterfields without interruption. Bob would sit beside me and smile, his eyes squinting and his lips curling as he talked in detail of the many people he had murdered. Elizabeth Taylor and other movie stars would tell him who his next victim would be.

My God, when I think back, how the hell was I there?

I would never become used to it, but I did learn how to retreat from it, just as I had learned to retreat from my mother.

A Mother's Love

With the screams, the smells, the cacophony, and the constant outbursts was violence. It was as regular and predictable as mealtime. I learned quickly how to avoid it as much as I could, but I would never get used to the sudden punches and lunges for my hair and face and the catlike scratching. One woman in particular would walk the hall with her hands raised stiffly over her head, dropping them on a cue only she could hear, and send a quick jab to a passing face. None of the staff did anything to stop her roaming or her violence.

My first night there was petrifying. Someone had quietly stolen my shoes after I had taken them off and turned my attention briefly to the raucous scenes unfolding in front of me. That first night, I was afraid to get out of bed, afraid to walk barefoot anywhere in that place.

I did not sleep that first night. The sharpness of the odors and the screams were far too unsettling. I would not sleep at night again until I left there, stealing naps during the comforting daylight when I could.

The one single light of that place came from the staff, almost to a person African American. In those days, in that area, racial equality was not even a concept. Times were tense, and racial lines were clear. Alton was only a short distance from Ferguson, Missouri, still a festering racial hotbed in 2015. Imagine it fifty years before. Like the security guard who led me in, the staff was cheerful, considerate, and maybe even sympathetic. It was odd that in that dark place I found the first kindness and support of my entire life. But it was fleeting and only occasional. There was only so much they could do.

But from that hell and the darkness I was immersed in for two years, those wonderful women gave me something I had never known—kindness and maybe even love.

Strange to have to go to a place like that to find my first kindness.

It was also odd that I found such affection from African Americans, a group for whom my mother reserved special contempt. One would think as a Native American who had felt prejudice herself, she would have been more open-minded. But it never did any good to apply logic to anything she did.

I met Vicki when I was shown the huge single room where everyone slept. My eyes were drawn immediately to the white metal beds, each with white metal headboards, more than one hundred lined neatly in six or seven rows, one after another. Vicki's was near mine, and I guess the appearance of some-one her age, who did not seem crazy, had attracted her almost immediately.

As she walked quickly up to me and said hello, I noticed what I thought was a man sitting next to a neatly made bed. He was talking to himself in a deep voice, opening his mouth widely as he spoke and leaning back into his chair, his long black hair falling onto the bed behind him. I noticed he had no teeth, and in those tense moments, I started to laugh. I'd never seen anything quite like that. I would quickly learn that it was a woman and that such things were far from unusual.

I would also learn very quickly nighttime was reserved for a spe-cial madness, and I would never in two years have a good night's sleep, especially in that large dormitory. People came alive at night it seemed, the noise increasing as darkness fell.

But again, I found another gesture of kindness on that first night. A man who worked the night shift noticed my terror and pushed my bed outside the main dormitory to a well-lit but quiet nurse's station across the hall. The morning staff would complain when they found me sleeping there, but he continued to move my bed each night.

Often, though, I still found it difficult to sleep, and I'd move into the dayroom and try to curl up on one of the chairs facing the blank television. There were still a lot of patients up and about, though, walking in their own private terrors. The cigarette-butt woman was always awake, walking, and smoking. She seemed obsessed with my shoes and would follow me each night, waiting for me to slip them off. She never tired of the game and never reacted when I snatched back my shoes and told her to stop.

Days were rigid and dully predictable. We stood in lines for our clothes, lines for our medicine, and lines for our food. Then we'd move to the dayroom, where we'd sit, staring at one another or the small television.

Each morning before breakfast, we lined up to get our day clothes, dispensed by a dour woman we called the linen lady, and then we moved on to get our medications. The dosing ritual never changed. Get to the nurses station, give your name, get the pills, and wash them down with juice. Then open our mouths for the nurse to show we had swallowed. The juice was another surprise for me. I had never tasted anything as sweet and refreshing as the juice, another bizarre first.

As the numbness of the medications took hold, we trudged to the cafeteria, where workers ladled out the day's inedible fare. Shit on a shingle, we called it.

We had no recreational programs, no insistence or encouragement from the staff to move, talk, or engage in anything. Day after numbing day, it was the same. People sat in drugged stupors in that dayroom, some drooling, others trying to make sense of the stream of babble from the television. That was my life.

The first time my mother came to visit, she screamed. Even in her own cold world, she had not imagined the horrors of Spruce Cottage. I never asked her, but I can only imagine she had thought that perhaps Alton would have been like Longview. I don't know. But by then, it was too late. I was a ward of the state and would stay.

My mother never once expressed guilt for it, for sending me to that place. In her twisted way, she quickly convinced herself that I was worse than even she thought, an evil child who deserved Spruce Cottage. I imagine she at some point congratulated herself for getting me into Alton before it was too late, for finding the cruel and bare hope I needed, as gruesome as it was. She was very likely upset with herself for not sending me there earlier. In the end, she quickly realized I deserved Spruce Cottage. She never apologized.

The strangest thing about the darkness and disconnection of Alton is that I would find and feel great kindness there, from the staff and nurse who genuinely felt my pain, who offered sympathy and even an occasional hug.

Funny that I'd have to go to a chaotic mental institution to find something close to love.

Jackie James Greer
Louise Greer her mother

Theresa left
Bettyrose right

Jackie Greer left
Right is a sister

Daddy

Grandma Woody
Daddy's mother

Nine

WONDERING

When I was three to five, I often wondered what it would be like to sit on my mother's lap in her warm embrace, maybe inhaling the kitchen sweetness of the nice dinner she had just cooked. I wondered what it might be like to have her sing me a lullaby as she tucked me into bed and kissed me good-night and wished me sweet dreams. I thought of how it might be if she walked me to school, holding my hand and telling me wonderful stories.

The only song my mother sang for me was a slow and uninterrupted dirge, a lament that I existed. The only thing I smelled was the stale smoke from the cigarettes she constantly smoked. The only thing she ever told me was that I was useless and a waste and a monster she wished she had never created.

When I was three to five, I did not want the screaming, the insults, and the paralyzing isolation. I certainly didn't want my mother's hatred. I wanted love, some faint wisp of love. That would have done wonders. At that age, I didn't sit back and analyze what was happening. I didn't think, *She's sick, my mother. She's mentally ill and needs help.* I absorbed that hate while I wondered about love.

Later, when in my thirties and well along the path of looking for love, I bought a *Diagnostic and Statistical Manual of Mental Disorders* for twenty-five cents at a yard sale. It opened my eyes, but it certainly didn't open my heart or inject me with a sudden knowing sympathy for my mother. As I read and thought back on my life with my mother, it all became clear to me in an academic, textbook sort of way. But textbooks and analysis can't convey the true dismal nature of the lives of people who live with narcissists.

It's not even close. As I read those clinical definitions, my mother emerged from the pages with stunning clarity. It explained many things to me, but it didn't make me feel any better. I still study that manual today, even after she's dead. I'm not sure why, to tell you the truth. I'm not sure what I'm looking for. Whatever it is, I haven't found it.

I spent most of my life looking for love because of that woman, and because of that, I hated her. My mother went to her grave without an apology. She had eight children and they all hated her. My mother died alone in a nursing home. That was not the Hollywood ending she had imagined for herself. It was not the way her movie was supposed to end.

My mother suffered from narcissistic personality disorder. She was a poster child for all its inherent disruption and havoc. Jackie Greer was a monster. She was an atomic explosion of hate, and the fallout from that hate is still wreaking havoc.

According to the Mayo Clinic, *Narcissistic personality disorder is a mental disorder in which people have an inflated sense of their own importance, a deep need for admiration, and a lack of empathy for others. But behind this mask of ultraconfidence lies a fragile self-esteem, vulnerable to the slightest criticism.*

My mother never pulled off her mask. To the world, she was a long-suffering heroic angel, doing so much with so little while having to deal with her troublesome children.

Narcissistic personality disorder causes problems with relationships, work, and managing finances. My mother was always disappointed with pretty much everything. She felt she was not getting the special favors or admiration she believed she deserved. She always felt superior to everyone and had an unquenchable sense of entitlement. She frequently belittled neighbors, relatives, and us, her children, of course. It never stopped.

When Jackie Greer didn't get what she wanted, she became angry. She was angry every waking hour of the day for her entire life. She was probably angry as she slept. Anger was her sustenance, what drove her and allowed her to survive. She could not deal with anything she perceived as criticism, and to avoid that, she created for the outside world, an image that certainly wasn't like anything we knew at home.

The official, clinical diagnosis for narcissistic personality disorder lists a number of clear items to qualify. As I read my yard sale manual, I felt as if they had used my mother as their case study. Someone with the condition has an exaggerated sense of self-importance. She will often expect to be recognized as superior even without achievements that warrant it. She will exaggerate her achievements and talents. She will also believe that because she is superior, she could be understood only by equally special people.

The list goes on, and the more I read, the more my mother emerged from the pages, clear and emphatic. These people are incapable of understanding the needs of others, and they take advantage of weaknesses to get what they want. They are arrogant and haughty.

It's fine and well to have that clinical definition, but that definition does not translate well to the things my mother did to us. It does give me something to lock onto. It helps me at least know it wasn't me whom she hated. Me alone, that is. She hated the world, and it wasn't my fault. I guess that's one small grace I got from understanding the problem.

My mother drew energy from the pain she washed over others. You could actually see and feel that, the boost she got as she screamed insults or pushed or tried to bring me down and into her control. She loved the reactions.

"You're a whore," she told me when I was five-years-old.

"You're a mistake."

"I will break you."

That was her favorite.

She said that to me throughout her life.

She broke my sister Jenny, and she enjoyed doing it—relished the fact that she was torturing Jenny. Jenny left home at ten and later moved in with a priest and had a child with him. I don't speak with Jenny these days, but I know all these years later my mother's legacy with Jenny is a life of heavy medication to get through the day. My mother would have loved that for me as well, I know.

She loved reactions, and I would not give her one. I locked in and refused to register the pain. That is what kept me strong, my ability to not react to her insults and abuse. That was my challenge, and I was up for it. But it locked my emotions in a place that took years to get out. That's how I have lived my life. I would not surrender my sanity to that woman. She told me once that I was born so she would have someone to torment. She actually said that to me. She often told me that by giving birth to me, she had created a monster. That was her cross to bear, her burden. She predicted that I would end up a drug addict or a whore.

That's another thing about narcissists, at least in my mother's case. Her projection for what I would become was actually a reflection of who she was. She used her attractiveness and her sexual charms to drag men into her life. Yet I was the one who would be a whore.

I later heard a definition that narcissists are people who will steal your wallet and then help you look for it. In their misshapen world, everyone else but them is evil. Everyone was a whore when my mother used sex to get what she wanted from men. It certainly worked with Ed, and we were pulled into the drama with him.

He stayed, and we had to stay with him as we moved from place to place. Narcissists are wolves in sheep's clothing, and Ed was so lonely he couldn't see a thing.

I was only three or four when my mother had my father locked up in Cincinnati, packed us all tightly in a car, and drove us all off with Ed. It was high drama for a young girl, to be sure. Ed was not a bad man, but he was lonely. My mother played that to the hilt. Ed had been in a bad marriage to a high school principal who paid no attention to him and eventually left him. Mother reeled him in and took us along for the ride. That's the power of a narcissist. And Ed never saw through the intricate charade and the games my mother played.

I believe that Ed thought Mother's behavior, the screaming, the breaking of dishes, and the chaos, was all somehow related to our father. He felt, from the distance he kept from us, that our behavior was not my mother's fault. He kept safe. She loved the drama.

I read in the manual with great interest another description: "A game for one has little gain for a narcissist, as they need to plug into someone else to receive an emotional fix. Narcissists are detached from their emotions as there are blockages preventing movement. The only way they are capable of processing emotions is when they tap into someone else's emotional energy."

Another textbook only confirmed what I was learning, and as I read it, my mother jumped from the page.

"Narcissistic personality disorder is a mental disorder in which people have an inflated sense of their own importance, a deep need for admiration and a lack of empathy for others. But behind this mask lies a fragile self-esteem that's vulnerable to the slightest criticism."

She would tell me, "I broke your father and I broke Jenny and I will break you."

There are now websites and support groups in the Facebook age. I take no comfort from some of the comments, but I recognize where they are coming from.

Things in the 1960s were not so open in Metropolis, Sayler Park, Cahokia, or Paducah. Besides, my mother could spin a tale so ridiculous in its incredibility that people would think, *That's so crazy it has to be true.* Funny how that works, but it did, no matter who Jackie Greer talked to or where we lived.

I did more research and found another piece that hit me hard, and I knew that unlike my mother, if I said anything about my life, explained even vaguely about my own private hell, no one would believe me.

I recognized this for sure:

"By the time we're ready to tell others of our abusive experience, we realize that the narcissist has preempted us and gotten their word out first. While we've been dealing with what we thought were real emotions and a real relationship, the narcissist has already strategized their exit plan. They get their words out: The words that we know intimately are nothing short of pathological lying and twisting revisionist history. The narcissist will tell others we're crazy, a stalker, vengeful, a poor loser, losers, or emotionally unstable. They'll site our reactions to their abuse as evidence, never mentioning the abuse that caused our reactions."

Some comments from a website bring back memories and give me some solace that I was not alone, but as I said, it doesn't do much good. I found a comment on one that rang true. My mother reserved a special place for me in her pool of bile. My sister Janie escaped that.

"Thank you. You get it. You know how it works. I'm not crazy. My mother is a narcissist, and I am her victim. My family stays on the sidelines because they don't want to get involved, and my sibling thinks everything can be resolved using a peaceful tone of voice. Well, she didn't grow up the scapegoat; I did. I was treated like garbage and she was coddled, so she doesn't understand."

Another comment rang true as well. "Perhaps telling our stories here is a good start to doing something. At least this site is a gathering place where those who have been through the damage can be heard and believed. It would be useful to make these stories as detailed as reasonably possible."

My mother did not want us around, but we were solid props in the movie she was creating. For me, as my mother often said, I was born to suffer, and she would make sure that was going to happen. That was my destiny, and she was my executioner. Narcissistic personality disorder does not leave room for compassion, logic, or any sense.

"You were meant to live a hell on earth, and that's my job, to make sure you do." She told me that until her final days.

Later, I found another online group for adult children of narcissistic parents that tried to make some sense of what I went through. Some things jumped out at me, as if my mother were standing in front of me, about to start in with her abuse and fiction.

"Narcissists believe everything they do is deniable. There is always a facile excuse or an explanation. Cruelties are couched in loving terms. Aggressive and hostile acts are paraded as thoughtfulness. Selfish manipulations are presented as gifts. Criticism and slander is slyly disguised as concern. She only wants what is best for you. She only wants to help you."

The description continued:

"Your accomplishments are acknowledged only to the extent that she can take credit for them. Any success or accomplishment for which she cannot take credit is ignored or diminished. Anytime you are to be center stage and there is no opportunity for her to be the center of attention, she will try to prevent the occasion altogether, or she doesn't come, or she leaves early, or she acts like it's no big deal, or she steals the spotlight or she slips in little wounding comments about how much better someone else did or how what you did wasn't as much as you could have done or as you think it is."

I read some comments from people on that website, and one jumped out at me. It certainly gave me some sense that I was not alone.

"The childhood of a person raised by a narcissistic parent is all kinds of horrible. The narcissist parent does not recognize the child as a separate human. The childhood of a narcissistic parent is a brutal one. And, unfortunately, due to the amount of psychological manipulation and abuse that the child is conditioned to accept, the abuse of the narcissistic parent often extends far into adulthood."

And another comment hit me hard:

"I remember when I was little, around 8 years old, I could rarely go to my friends', and no one was allowed in our house. She would hit me with a belt, laying down on the bed with my pants down (I knew in advance though how many slaps for every bad manner) and she would say that I was lucky because she was hit with the buckle when she was little (Remember, she always suffered more)."

That, I guess, was what was called validation. I learned that I was not the only one to go through that special hell, and I did not cause it. No one ever asked me what I wanted. If they had, I had an answer ready. I wanted love.

Ten

July

Nearly fifty years after the blackest day of my life, a hot, horrid Cincinnati day in July, I still shut down for the entire month. The whole time I feel like I'm trapped underwater and being pulled farther down by an undertow I cannot escape. I can't catch my breath.

Every year as the anniversary of that day approaches, I can feel myself pulling away from daily life as the memories close in. I can't shake them. I slam the door and keep it closed all month long. I've been doing so for as long as I can remember because the jagged memories are simply too much. I don't hear my telephone in July. I never pick it up to make a call. I don't enjoy a single thing I eat. A psychiatrist might tell you I'm disassociating from the trauma, stepping away from it, trying to forget something so horrid and repellant it is embedded in everything I do. I can't get away from it.

But every July, I do step away. I won't go outside or engage in conversations if I can get away with it. I stay away from the neighbors. I try to get off work as much as possible, and I'll pay my July bills in June if I have to. Loved ones know that and let me settle into my own darkness. I want nothing to do with July and its celebrations, sunshine, fireworks, summer picnics, and fun trips to the lake.

Nothing.

I was raped twice in July when I was eleven-years-old, on the same night, by two different men. In a life of having innocence and hope slowly squeezed from me by my mother, that was the night I surrendered it totally. I can clearly draw the line when the suffocating violence of those rapes pulled from me my life, and hope, and any light I was still conscious of. That night left an ugly, fetid wound in a darkness so thick no light will ever penetrate it. There is no redemption or hard lessons learned or hope. Just hell.

Before that night I wanted love and knew vaguely how it worked because I did have moments of love and light, even living with my mother and her darkness. But that ended that night. And for fifty years, it has paralyzed me each July. There are times I feel I can't find the fresh air that will sustain me, though I do.

By age eleven, I had become used to moving, and by that July, we were back in Cincinnati. We'd been living our disconnected lives in Cahokia with Ed, but my mother pulled up stakes again and returned to Sayler Park, the neat suburb where I had been born and where we had lived until I was three, as a family with my father.

My father was an industrious man, always working. At one point, he owned a restaurant, and a laundromat called Lou's. We lived in an apartment in the building above the restaurant and laundromat. Things seemed fine at that point, but I was young and unaware of the undercurrents between my parents. I was too young to understand my mother's need for constant attention and her way with men.

She had worked her charms on my father, that's for sure. He was a quiet man and hardworking. When he met my mother, he was already married, but she was so magnetic and charming that he became lost in her charm. But he would soon learn that Jackie

A Mother's Love

Greer was no one to trifle with, and he was smart enough to step away. But he still loved her.

When I was nine or ten, I found a letter he had written asking her to return, to come back and start over again—to leave Ed and give the kids a chance. But by that time, she had charmed Ed and probably many others.

During one of my mother's times away from Ed, my sister Janie and I would sneak in and read Ed's letters to her, filled with wanting and lust and the need to see her and to be with her, maybe even in her black negligee.

Mom had meet Ed at my father's restaurant, and when I was three-years-old, they took off together, uprooting us and taking off across the Midwest, while Ed followed his job as an accountant with Ferlin-Collins. They moved us to Metropolis, then Paducah, then Cahokia. My mother was like that, able to use her sex and her beauty to get men to do what she wanted. I'm not sure how many men she had attracted that way. Ed always stayed around, no matter how many times she left him. Ed was the only sucker. It is impossible to understand my mother's motivations, other than to know that whatever she did was always about her, regardless of the suffering she inflicted on those around her.

When I was eleven, my mother finally decided to divorce my father, to end the charade that Ed was her brother that she'd been carrying around in the various places we had lived. So in her mad logic, she left Ed, packed us up again, and moved back to Cincinnati. When the divorce from my father was final, she would marry Ed, she thought. So one morning in Cahokia, Ed went to work, and my mother said we were moving. She and a neighbor packed the truck. And we were off to Cincinnati.

I had liked Ohio—I'd been born in Cincinnati—and had fond memories of living there before my mother and Ed uprooted us.

Bettyrose Woody

So at eleven, I was back in Cincinnati, living in a two-story white stucco house with blue trim. In the tangled web she weaved so efficiently, my father was still connected. He had built that house in Sayler Park at Gracely Drive. I remember the long driveway, the swimming pool beside it, and the detached garage. The blue swimming pool had large square blue-and-pink pavers. The pool was painted the same color as the trim of the house and garage. It was neat, orderly, and comforting, so very different from our lives.

In the bizarre sentimentality my mother had, despite her constant cruelty, she loved Sayler Park and remembered a statue there of a Native American—one of her people. Years later, when I was an adult and free of her, she wrote me after a tornado had passed through town. Was the statue still standing? she asked. She never told us we were part Native American, but she often spoke of Indians. Whenever she would see a feather, she would comment what it meant. If she saw a tree that had been bent, she would comment that was how Indians marked their way. She spoke of different ways the Indians made paint with the juice of berries, and she always donated clothes and coats to the Native Americans.

She hated the cold and always pointed out to us that the Indians were freezing and starving to death. Whenever she saw some stranger in need, she always stopped to help them. She was always kind to strangers. That was the bizarre thing about my mother, her isolated and disjointed feelings; her apparent love for those faceless Native Americans and her very real hatred for her children.

Being back in Sayler Park was at first comforting. I was happy to be near my father again and thought it was in many ways a blessing. But even then, as the high summer heat of southern Ohio began to increase and the humidity began to close in, we all knew it was going to end, and probably soon. My mother was divorcing my father, and we would soon be back in Cahokia with her and Ed. No matter where we lived, life with my mother would remain terrifying. We all knew that. But the wedding was set, and the night before, as my mother headed off to her sister-in-law's to have her hair done, we were all on edge.

It was a somber night, to be sure. We knew we'd soon be back in Cahokia with Mom and Ed, and this time there would be no pretending he was her brother. I had never liked Cahokia and the falseness of the life, of having to pretend Ed was our uncle. The next time would all be formal and official. I felt there was no escape. My hope that my parents would get back together was about to end.

Before she went off to have her hair done, my mother called Janie inside and screamed at her. It didn't really matter what Janie had failed to do because our mother screamed for any reason. That night, it was because Janie had not done the dishes as she had been told to do. My mother beat her with some frozen sausages that had been sitting conveniently on the counter. I was crying outside but happy in a way that this time it was Janie being punished. Usually it was me.

I heard my mother calling, and I knew I would be next. I ran behind the house, then into the neighbor's backyard, where I hid in the shrubbery, and I watched as my mother called and screamed my name. When she left for her hair appointment, I started walking, not sure where I was going, knowing only that I had to get away. I soon found myself in front of Lou's Drugstore, which was right down the street from our house.

Lounging around outside was an older teenage boy I recognized. He often hung around there with a friend.

"Your mom's looking for you," he told me.

"I want to go to my father's," I told him, oblivious to his looks and certainly his intentions.

I was eleven. I doubt very much I weighed one hundred pounds at the time. He was probably seventeen, strong and developed. I got into his car. Instead of taking me to my father's, he drove to his parents' house. He stopped outside, and as he parked the car, he told me his parents were in Florida.

"Do you want to go in?" he asked.

"Fine," I said.

My memory comes in brief flashes after that, of violence and unfathomable wrenching horror. I had no idea what happened. I remember walking into the house. I can still picture his parents' bedroom and the thick carpet. I can remember how soft it was.

I remember him hurriedly and roughly pulling down my short pants and his silence as he pulled me to the floor. My pants were blue, I remember. I recall the pain and how powerless I was to stop what he was doing to me. I had no idea what was happening, only that it was violent, horrid, and wrong.

He said nothing, and when he finished, I sat stunned as he told me he'd take me to my father's apartment. I did not know what to say. I could not begin to comprehend what had just happened. He dropped me off at my father's apartment in silence. There were no explanations or apologies. Nothing.

I have no idea how late it was, how much time had passed. Time meant nothing, but it must have been late. As he drove off, I walked down the short alleyway to my father's place and looked in the window. I saw my brother sleeping there in the summer heat. There was no air conditioning in those days.

I was in another world. Shocked, trying to grasp what the boy had just done to me. A strong teenage boy had raped me in his mother's bed. How do I explain that—explain the unexplainable? I did not know how to react, how to feel, what to say. How do I explain such indescribable horror to my father or brother or, God forbid, my mother?

On the eve of her own special occasion?

I didn't know what to do, other than I needed to walk to try to figure out what had happened.

A Mother's Love

So I started walking.

That area of Cincinnati is hilly—in fact, it is known as the Seven Hills—and lacing those hills are dozens of staircases, each with hundreds of steps, leading from a lower street to the one above. The area is hilly and wooded. During the day, in the bright light, the area is pleasant and charming—a bit of the woods in the suburbs.

At night, it is a different matter, though. There was nothing inviting, charming, or safe at night. I knew nothing but the horrors of what had just been done to me, and I was incapable of sensing any danger. I was in shock and didn't know how to react or what to do. I was paralyzed.

I couldn't go to my mother's, certainly. I couldn't explain to my brother or father, to anyone, what had happened. I sat on the steps. Lost. I had no idea what time it was.

A man appeared and asked me what I was doing, sitting on the step so late and so lonely. He talked to me, and he kept talking. I didn't say a thing. I didn't offer a clue to anything, but my vulnerability and isolation must have been clear and open.

Then he threw me to the ground at the base of those steps, and he raped me. Violently. Like I was a piece of trash that had somehow become trapped on that isolated stairway. I was in complete and chaotic darkness, in a hell I did not know existed four hours before. Then the man left without saying a word.

I sat there until daylight in stunned and terrified silence. I'm not sure how long I was there or what finally prompted me to move, but I did and somehow made it to a friend's house. I knocked on the door and asked if I could sit for a while. I explained nothing. I have explained nothing for fifty years. Until now.

I write this only in hopes that it will help someone, that someone else who might be suffering now will know that it is possible to spend time in hell and return to life; scarred maybe but alive nonetheless.

Alive and hopeful.

I stayed at my friend's house that morning, not talking but wrapped in some sense of comfort that I was away from the horrors of the night before, but by then, my mother had reported me missing. I told her nothing. She told me I had ruined her wedding.

Eleven

MISSING

I did not attend my mother and Ed's wedding. My absence did not lead to a frantic search or a last-minute postponement of the ceremony. Ed and my mother tied the knot without too much disruption.

I know there was at last some acknowledgment that I wasn't there, at least a bit of a nod to my disappearance. Later, my mother told me I had ruined the wedding. She would never stop reminding me of that.

I think they had only a vague sense I wasn't there. At the time, I didn't care to hear what I missed on the grand occasion, whether there was laughter and dancing and drinks and music. Knowing my mother and Ed, I suppose there was. Nothing as trivial as a missing child was going to stop those two from indulging themselves.

After my own hellish, brutal night, I was so numb I didn't have any idea what I wanted, what had happened, or what I should do. I had been reduced to a fragile shell by those attacks. I was shattered. I walked in a vacuum, without emotion, or thought, or anything that remotely resembled feeling or understanding. I assume

I simply reacted to the one glimmer of warmth in our neighborhood, which pulled me toward the Mattinglys.

In those days, the mid-1960s, neighborhoods still had some vestige of permanence. Families had lived in Sayler Park side by side for generations. Everyone knew everyone else, and that went back for years. It was a much closer time than today, where neighbors rarely even nod at one another, if they even know their neighbors at all.

I was used to moving, so I moved. I could not sit on those horrid steps any longer than I did. That morning as the sun slowly spread its warmth over Sayler Park, I numbly made my way to the Mattinglys' house. I saw no light and felt no warmth that morning. But I knew the loud, loving, and raucous Mattingly family would take me in. And I knew I would be lost there for as a long as I cared to be.

The Mattinglys were a huge family, children of all ages coming and going at all times of the day. My grandmother had been friends with one or another generation of the Mattinglys for years, and they knew my father well.

I made my way to the front door of the Mattinglys' huge house. I'm certain I must have asked if I could stay there, but I'm not sure. I told one of the Mattingly girls I needed to hide from everyone, including my mother, father, sisters, and brothers. I told her I needed a place to stay for a while. I did not tell her why, and she did not ask.

Her parents had already left for work, and she took me in. She was always helping strays from the neighborhood. She brought me to the third floor, where there were three empty bedrooms, with the beds fully made up. It was comfortable there at a time I needed some sense of comfort while I tried to register what had happened to me. I'm still trying to register what had happened even now, fifty years later, but certainly my stop at the Mattinglys provided some sense of security.

I was still in shock. I'm not even sure which of the Mattingly girls helped me. But after she brought me upstairs, she began to bring me meals. I ate mechanically, barely at all. I had no appetite. I slept.

I did not leave that room except to use the third-floor bathroom. And no one questioned my presence, if they even knew I was there at all. There were so many kids coming and going out of that house that no one ever gave my presence a second thought.

My mother thought I had run away, but she really did not care enough to stop the wedding, or to look too hard, or to disrupt her life. Eventually, she found me. The same closeness that made Price Hill so attractive also meant that there were very few secrets.

After I was at the Mattinglys for about a week, making a rare appearance downstairs and talking to some of the other Mattingly children, I guess word got out where I was. One afternoon, my mother and Ed showed up. And they brought the police with them.

One would normally expect that a concerned, maybe even frantic, mother and her new husband would bring the police along. They would be concerned and worried and want to make sure I was all right. That was not the driving force behind my mother's showing up with Ed and the police at the Mattinglys' front door.

Behind her false concern was the fact that my mother needed her child support checks from my father. With me missing or staying at the Mattinglys', she wouldn't get the check. That was really what it was all about. She was motivated by money, not emotion, or love, or anything close to it.

She put on her act for the benefit of the Mattinglys and the police. The concerned, loving mother act was an effective tool she had always been able to use. Why, she asked, had I disappeared? Why had I done so the night before her wedding? Why had I hated her so much that I would do such a horrible thing?

I was still in shock from the horrors of that night that had sent me to the Mattinglys. I was still trying to process what had happened. It was futile, of course. Eleven-year-old girls are supposed to be processing things like a bad day at school, or a bad grade on a test, or her soccer team's loss. Those were the sorts of things an eleven-year-old should have been dealing with, not being violently raped twice on the same night.

I told them what happened as best I could, why I had run away. Why I was hiding at the Mattinglys'.

I still did not understand what had happened. I was still in shock.

After hearing my attempt to describe what had happened, the police deemed me a runaway and took me to juvenile hall while they investigated.

Juvenile hall was a violent, shocking, and unforgiving place for a shell-shocked eleven-year-old. What had I done? I wasn't sure, but I knew I was being punished for it. The place was dirty and noisy and anything but safe. It was a warehouse for the unwanted and the angry. Kids there tortured one another mercilessly. Older kids sought out the younger. Stronger kids looked for the weaker. Adult supervisors looked on, not caring to get involved.

It was certainly not a haven or a place of refuge for eleven-year-old rape victims. But juvenile hall was my reward for being raped. While I was there, I was tested. I was pregnant. Eleven-years-old.

After a week of the hell that was juvenile hall, I went with my parents to court for a custody hearing while the criminal matter of the rapes was investigated. My mother was not concerned about the rapes.

She told the judge what she had repeatedly told my father. The rapes showed precisely what I was, and what she had been saying I was: an evil child, a child unworthy of her love and devotion. I was a whore, she said.

But being the concerned mother that she was, she told the judge she wanted me back to at least to provide me with the love and care I needed. My mother's lying was on its best display.

A Mother's Love

She did not mention that I had run from her that night to escape her screaming and the beating that would likely follow. She did not mention that she had beaten Janie; that she often beat her children. No, that somehow did not come out when she was speaking so earnestly to the judge—this loving, caring, misunderstood mother who needed her child.

My father was upset about my situation, of course, but he had heard my mother's stories about me so often that I think he was uncertain of my situation. Had I somehow brought all this on myself? He had not spent a lot of time with me, and maybe she had planted just a small seed of doubt. The situation was so horrible—an eleven-year-old pregnant? Running around by herself at night? He was upset and, I suppose, shocked.

The judge saw right through my mother and did so quickly. He was, I suppose, used to charades and lying in family court. He was probably numb to such fake pleadings of innocence and love. He was wise enough to ask for a simple exercise. Looking at me from the bench, he asked me to walk to each of my parents and give them a hug.

I went first to my mother, who was sitting in a chair along the wall of the small hearing room. She did not get up as I stood in front of her. When I tried to put my arms around her, she flinched and sat back rigid and stiff. I suppose she was fighting that cold reaction that she was trying to show for the judge her love. She could not do it, though, try as she might. Showing physical affection was too much an act, even for that veteran actress.

Next, I went to my father. He stood, then he wrapped his arms around me, covering me with a warm, forgiving embrace. My father was a man to be demonstrable in his affection. He began to tear up but said nothing.

The judge ruled I would go to my father. I did so with no small amount of relief. At the time, my father lived across the street from the police department. That proved to be convenient for the investigators. Shortly after I had settled into my father's apartment, two detectives came to interview me.

As I look back on it now, those two men must have been totally perplexed at their assignment—an eleven-year-old girl, pregnant, raped in the neighborhood, or at least claiming to have been raped. It was likely they had never had a case like that. It is also likely they had no idea of even where to start. They took me for a drive.

Where did the boy live? they asked.

I showed them.

Where did he pick you up?

I showed them.

I also showed them Lou's Pharmacy, where the boy often hung out. I told them what he had said about his mother's new carpet. I showed them everything, including the bushes where I had hidden from my screaming mother. I told them what he did to me, as much as I could understand, anyway. It was clear they did not know how to react. This was a neighborhood boy from a neighborhood family.

There would never be any charges filed. I'm not certain why. I'm not certain what the police decided or how they decided it. Did they think I had somehow provoked the incident? Did they think I had made it up, that I had somehow imagined this glimpse of hell? That I had caused the whole thing and I was now trying to escape by making up such a fantastic story? I don't know, and I never will.

I'm not certain, even today, if a new car my father got was somehow tied to money from the boy's family. Much later, many years after the fact, I tried to file charges, to reopen the investigation. The boy is now a well-known figure in the area. It was too late. The statute of limitations had expired.

After the police had made their superficial investigation and did little else, my father took me to a gynecologist for a second examination. Perhaps he thought the results of the quick one at juvenile hall was a mistake. Maybe he prayed that his eleven-year-old daughter was not pregnant. Maybe things had just gotten mixed up.

A second examination showed I was pregnant. My father asked about an abortion and was told it was illegal. He asked if there was a way to induce a miscarriage, looking for a way around the situation. I'm not sure what the doctor's answer was. I don't blame my father at all. I know he was trying to help.

Soon after our visit with the gynecologist, I had a miscarriage. I'm not sure if it was somehow related to our visit with the doctor. I had gone into the bathroom at one point, feeling uneasy, a bit queasy. My stomach was cramping. As I sat doubled over in the bathroom, it felt as if my insides suddenly gushed out. It was a spasm of pain and a forceful voiding. I was frightened and shocked.

I ran to my father in the other room, crying that something bad had just happened. He walked to the bathroom and stared. Without a word, I watched as he reached in and pulled a small solid glob from inside. He said nothing. He would put it in a bottle of alcohol. He immediately called an ambulance, and I was rushed to the hospital, where doctors confirmed I had had a miscarriage. I was devastated.

After all the talk about being pregnant, I had decided I wanted a baby. I wanted someone who would love me unconditionally. Love was in such short supply in Sayler Park in those days.

Twelve

Still in shock, frozen, I guess, I was admitted to the hospital after my miscarriage. I was dazed and despondent and once again in a place I chose not to be. That I had been pregnant at eleven-years-old was beside the larger point. I certainly did not understand what had happened or exactly what being pregnant meant. But I knew at a basic level that inside me I had a child I could shower with love, someone I could give everything I never had. In a very dark way, it was almost magical. The miscarriage ended that innocent hope.

While I was at the hospital, I saw something rare. It was a brief flash of kindness from the staff, who no doubt was shocked by this young waif of a girl in their care after a miscarriage. Sitting in my room, alone, I was ambivalent about life itself, about all that had happened in the past month, once again drifting into my place of retreat, the place where I too often went in those times.

An older man walked in. He was wearing a white hospital coat and had a stethoscope clamped around his neck. He smiled and asked how I was feeling, if I needed anything. He reassured me that everything would be fine and that I would be going home in short order. He told me to rest, eat, and try to relax and put away any bad thoughts.

I wasn't quite sure what to make of this man. I realized he was trying to be kind, that he was concerned and actually worried about me. He left, giving me a gentle pat on my back and a smile.

"Everything will be fine," he said. "Don't worry." The nurses who cared for me over the next day were the same: gentle, accommodating, and concerned.

I had never experienced anything like it. I was so accustomed to my mother and her steady violence and abuse that I was almost stunned by the gentleness and the concern of the staff at that hospital. I was treated as a human being, a poor child who had been so violated, so damaged, that I needed their care. They showed it, and I will never forget their kindness. To them, I was a young patient who had seen far too much. To me, they were bearers of something I had never experienced.

I learned later that while I was in the hospital, my father had approached the detectives who had been questioning me and told them he was dropping the charges against my rapist. I was stunned to hear the news. To this day, I don't know why. But my father soon had a new car, and my tormentor was out of the work farm as if nothing had ever happened. The whole violent incident was seemingly forgotten by everyone but me.

My father and I would return to the kind doctor at his office for another appointment in short order. He and his wife, who I would guess was also a doctor, sat with my father and me and confirmed that I had indeed had a miscarriage. The thought that my rapist was free and the confirmation that I would not be having a baby were too much. It was a tipping point, as they say, like the proverbial straw that broke the camel's back.

We returned to my father's apartment in uneasy silence. I was drowning in confusion—the miscarriage, the dropped charges, the indifference of everyone. I retreated once again into myself and did what would become a pattern for me.

Bettyrose Woody

I was upset, numb, and unable to digest what was going on. I was being asked to simply brush it aside, to pretend nothing had happened. I couldn't do that.

My father loved me, and I think he loved me deeply. He put me on a pedestal, which I enjoyed. But it was always fleeting, that comfort. After the rape, he was angry with me, and it seemed like a mute but powerful anger, as senseless as that might seem. In my father's mind, the entire incident somehow became my fault. It seemed that no one knew how to react; not the police, not my mother or father, and certainly not Ed, who didn't react to anything other than my mother's bullying.

I left my father's apartment, crossed the street, and started walking, slowly but deliberately to a destination I had pursued before—away. I wanted to be away from everything, and I did not care where away was. I had no idea where I was going or what I would do. I knew only that away was as safe a place as I could be.

I remember crossing a bridge, although I could not tell you the bridge or the river it crossed or the direction I was headed. I must have looked as aimless as I felt because as soon as I crossed the bridge and the noise of the city's business began to fade, a carful of young men pulled to the side of the road and stopped beside me.

I kept walking, but one of the young men, I'd guess they were in their late teens, rolled down the car's window and from the back seat asked where I was going.

"I don't know," I said.

"Want a ride?" he asked.

"Sure," I said as he opened the rear door of the car and the three boys in the back seat shuffled over to let me in.

The driver said they were heading to Peoria for work. Peoria meant nothing to me, but it sounded fine. I wanted to be anywhere other than where I was. Away from Sayler Park, Cincinnati, Cahokia, or anywhere else I had lived sounded fine to me. Any place but where I was.

A Mother's Love

Peoria was hours away, although I did not know that when I slid into the back seat. And as it turned out, the boys in the car were actually pretty nice. I certainly looked older than my eleven years, and I'm sure they thought the idea of having an attractive girl in the car with them for the long ride seemed a good idea, something different. They meant no harm and did not have dark intentions. They were just a bunch of kids out for a drive, really.

It's almost 350 miles northwest from Cincinnati to Peoria, all the way across Indiana and half of Illinois. It's a rural drive through miles of nothingness, just a brief flash of city through Indianapolis and then more nothingness, farm field, and flatness. I liked the thought of nothingness, of being somehow suspended between a "here" I hated and a "there" I didn't want to arrive at. The five hours of nothingness in that car with those boys was fine with me. I was not nervous, frightened, or worried. I certainly was not concerned that my mother would be worried where I was, that I had run off yet again.

Peoria is a city in the middle of a state in the middle of the country. It has often been cited as the prototypical emblem of Middle America: "Will it play in Peoria?" Of course, I did not know that, and I would not have cared if I did. It was just someplace other than where I was.

I did not know where Peoria was. I just sat in the back seat of the car with those boys, listening as they joked and sang along with the radio and tried to impress me with their worldliness. One of the boys seemed to be the leader of the group. I remember his name was Roy. Whatever town we passed through, Roy knew something about it, knew people there, or had once stayed there or had relatives there. He never stopped talking for the entire ride. That was fine with me. I needed all the distractions I could absorb, and Roy's chatter was funny and entertaining.

I did know only one thing: I was hungry. As we drove, I saw, one after another, billboards with enticing photos and advertisements for Kentucky Fried Chicken. They were everywhere. I thought, for some reason, we were in Kentucky, not that it mattered. I knew nothing of the geography of where I was and where we were going. I didn't care.

The boys were headed to Peoria to work on a construction job, although I'm not certain exactly what they did. They had made the trip before and had a small, almost primitive little shack they lived in while doing whatever it was they did. When we pulled up the unpaved road leading to the cottage, they insisted I stay with them, because it had become clear by then I was running way from something. I guess they sensed something was off because I had not gone into any great detail.

When we all walked inside, they began strewing their bags, equipment, and tools onto the floor, everyone staking out a place to sleep before they started work again in the morning. There was no water and no electricity. I guess it was just a place to sleep while they were in town doing whatever it was they did.

In the course of scrambling for floor space, one of the boys eventually asked me how old I was. I'm not sure why, maybe it was the excitement of having a girl stay with them for the night. When I told them I was eleven, everything changed. Even the talkative Roy was silent. It quickly became clear to them that they might be in big trouble, bringing an eleven-year-old across three states to their little Peoria shack. It was not something they wanted to be involved in, obviously. They quickly became nervous.

They seemed to be familiar enough with the area, and as soon as I told them, Roy quickly bundled me back in the car and drove me to a trailer park, where Roy knocked on a door and went inside. When he came out, a woman was with him, and she took my hand and brought me inside her cluttered but warm mobile home. I did not know who she was, and no one explained, but it was clear Roy and the young construction crew no longer wanted the attractive young girl they had found walking by the roadside in Cincinnati.

The middle-aged woman knew the boys and was some sort of relative, I guess, maybe an aunt. I'm not sure, but when Roy escorted me to the door of the trailer, he said something to her I could not hear and left. She invited me inside but said nothing. Then she picked up the phone and called the police.

After about twenty minutes of silence, a ruddy-faced police officer came to the door, talked briefly to the woman, took my hand, and escorted me to his cruiser, which was still running outside in the trailer's short driveway. He told me he was a friend of Roy and the other boys, that he had known them for years. He told me not to worry and that he would take care of me. He smiled as he reached into his glove compartment and sprayed some sort of breath freshener in his mouth. Then he pulled me close to him and tried to kiss me.

I instantly reached for the door handle and jumped outside, then ran as fast as I could down the trailer park road to the highway thirty yards away. The policeman did not try to follow.

I began walking as darkness slowly settled over the area. Once again, I was running. Once again, I had no idea where, but the motion was somehow comforting. With an occasional glace behind me to check that the policeman was not following, I turned and stood on the side of the road and stuck out my thumb.

I remember it was freezing, and I remember exactly what I was wearing: culottes covered by a short jumper with yellow pockets. I'm sure at one point for another young girl in another situation it would have been a cute outfit. There was nothing cute about my situation, and the only thing I knew as I stood on the side of the road was that I was cold.

As I stood there, alone, I also began to realize I was hungry and thirsty. God knows how long it had been since I had eaten anything. The first car to pass slowed, then stopped abruptly. Was it out of concern for the tiny young girl incongruously standing on the side of the road without a coat as the cold and darkness settled in? I actually think so.

The driver was older, although I don't really know what that meant. Everyone was old to me. Everyone was suspect. I had learned years before to not trust anyone. But he was around my father's age from the looks of it. I'm not sure if he was stunned by my appearance, by such a young kid hitchhiking, but he said little other than I looked cold and that I should not be hitching.

He drove me to his apartment in what looked like the center of town, telling me I should eat and warm up. He pointed to the bathroom and told me to take a bath and get cleaned up. As he did so, a woman who must have been his wife or girlfriend stood open-mouthed but said nothing.

While I was in the tub, with the warmth of the water just beginning to sink through my numbness, both physical and emotional, it began.

"What are you doing? What's wrong with you? Are you trying to get arrested? What the hell are you thinking?"

It went on without interruption, and he did not reply.

I got dressed as the yelling continued, and when I stepped outside, still damp but certainly cleaner and warmer, I heard, "Get that kid out of here."

He took me by the hand and brought me back outside to his car.

At that point, I knew I was facing two things I did not want to face. I knew I would have to go back to my father's, and eventually my mother's. That's how it always went. I had been trying to ignore that end result by running, by closing down, but I knew where I'd end up, and it did not appeal to me.

The man drove to a diner and bought me a cheeseburger and some fries, which I ate quickly, gulping down a Coke with it. Then he gave me ten dollars for a bus ticket back to Cincinnati. He knew I needed help but seemed puzzled about how to provide it. I guess giving me the money made sense to him, but as I think about it now, I wonder why he didn't simply pick up the phone and call my father. He did not ask me any details about why I was standing by the road, and I did not offer any.

Fewer complications, I guess.

I remember getting on a bus as the man watched. But the pressure and the chaos of that week has blurred what happened next. The next week flashes by in bits to me now.

I was headed east, I know, because the man had told me to go back to my father. I remember Indiana, although I'm not even sure where. Was it Indianapolis? Maybe. It actually does not really matter. Somehow, on that bus, the thought of going back to Cincinnati, of going back to Cahokia and my mother and Ed, drowned me, overwhelmed me. I got off the bus in a large city, that much I know.

I remember George Wallace, the governor of Alabama, was making his first renegade run for president of the United States, and I remember him making a speech to a crowd. He seemed to attract a mix of emotions. Some people sang his praises. Others tried to shout him down.

I remember the flower children in those beginning days of what would be the free-roaming days of hippies who traveled lightly and easily. I suppose a young girl on her own would not call too much attention to herself in those days. I remember a man with long hair and a feather in his floppy cap. I see flashes of couples with young children, infants, asking for handouts.

Mostly, though, and it is as clear as if he is sitting here right now, I remember an older black man in a wheelchair at the bus station where I got off. Sitting next to him was another ragged-looking old man. In front of them was a box, and as people walked by, the men asked for help, for money, for anything. I noticed people as they passed by, never turning to look at the vagabonds but unable to not do something. Most people tossed coins in the box.

I caught their attention, and they called me over. I was puzzled. "People will just give you money?" I asked.

They told me to sit next to them and see. "Just ask," they said.

So I did, and soon enough, passersby were dropping pennies and nickels and an occasional quarter into a cup I held as I asked.

I was mortified, humiliated. I was begging for money. But I was also hungry and did not want to go home, wherever that was. I felt degraded, but then. I was already degraded. It was just another degree of hell in my life. So I stayed at that bus station.

That night, I followed the others who were seeking warmth and the kindness of strangers into the large bathroom. It smelled, and it was damp and loud. But it was warm, and the others huddled in corners, trying to make it through the night into the next morning, when they would do it all over again.

Occasionally, a policeman would enter that bathroom, bang his stick on the walls and the stalls, and roust everyone out. We would file slowly back into the main hall of the bus station. When the policeman left, we would head back to the bathroom.

I stayed in that limbo for two days, not wanting to be there, not wanting to go to Cincinnati, Cahokia, or anywhere.

I guess I needed the warmth of the bus station bathroom, but I don't remember feeling cold. I guess I needed nutrition, because I remember buying food at a snack bar, even though I never felt hungry. I was numb to everything.

I knew, though, that normal forces would intervene, and I knew I would be pulled back into the stream. I knew the stream would never stop pulling me along, never allow me to get out. My mother needed her social security checks and at some point would try to find me. My father would be powerless to stop her, would never make an effort to fight her or try to keep me.

My mother was too strong, and fighting her was too exhausting. No one could, and no one ever did. They just ran away or rolled over and took her abuse. I knew, sitting in that bus station bathroom, that I would soon be back in Cahokia. I knew it was just a matter of time.

Thirteen

RUNNING

Away.
That was always my favorite destination. There was rarely a time when I was content enough, comfortable and at ease enough, to say to myself, I think I will stick around here for a while.

My stay at the bus station was certainly not one of those times. I was constantly cold and continuously embarrassed by the panhandling and the near-sleepless nights in the large and noisy bathroom, trying to get enough sleep between police raids. The odd thing about those few soiled days is that I was part of a community that in some bizarre way cared for me. I was protected, advised, and taught how to survive by those homeless people. In a way, they had adopted me. Those few days were certainly better than any time I spent with my mother.

It was inevitable that at some point I would be rousted for the last time. I was too young-looking, despite how the wear of the past month had aged me. Eventually, during one of the nightly clearances, a policeman noticed my smallness, placed his hands on my shoulders, and looked closely at my face. He pulled me aside as he forced the others out into the cold and dark street.

"You're coming with me," he told me as he took my arm and led me away, first to his patrol car, then to the station. I remember how nice it felt to be inside a warm car. I remember the softness of the seat, its vague comfort after days of hard floors and invading chills. But I also remember the grip of fear that was settling in alongside the warmth. It was overwhelming.

I knew I'd be going back to Cahokia and to my mother and Ed. As much as I ran, that was always the end result: my mother and her viciousness.

First, there was always the running, then the detention centers and their chaos and violence, followed by my mother's screaming and insults. It had become a predictable part of my life. No matter how much or how far I ran, the end result was always the same.

Literature on narcissists emphasizes that they are not capable of human emotion, not in even the remotest sense. As the world revolves around them, in their minds anyway, love, regret, and sympathy do not exist. Narcissists are like zombies. They feel nothing. My mother was not torn by my frequent and predictable runs from her. If she felt anything, my absences prompted regret that she no longer had me around to torture. She would have hated that gap, even though among her children I was the only one who never responded to her. But that did not prevent her from trying. She attempted her entire life to have me show some sign that she had frightened or cowed me. She wanted a reaction, and my refusal to give her one must have tormented her. I took no solace from that. She did have my sisters, though, in my frequent absences.

My mother was monster, and with her many children she had many minds to torture. My sisters reacted, unlike me. That gave my mother complete ecstatic satisfaction. I'm sure while I was gone she went after my youngest sister, Jenny. She would terrorize Jenny with dolls, throwing them at her, mocking her, frightening her with those toys. She would shake them in Jenny's mortified face. Jenny was petrified of the dolls, those mocking dolls. Soon enough, she also began running away. And like me, even today, Jenny is still running way, still mortified by the scars left by those dolls. Jenny would just melt, and that was the reaction that my mother loved.

With my older sister, Janie, it was spiders. Spiders paralyzed her, made her freeze in terror. Naturally, my mother would find a spider and toss it in her face or pretend she saw one and tell Janie it was looking for her. My mother loved the menace and the terror she could provoke with her ominous, implied threat that somehow Janie was about to die a painful death. More than anything, she loved the reactions and the fear, the total control she had over those young and once sweet and innocent minds.

With me, it was knives, or at least she tried to make it knives. I did not care and did not react when she would take a kitchen knife and bring it quickly to my face or threaten to run me through or cut my throat. She hated that I did not react. I never reacted. I never showed fear. I never let her control me with her terrors. I suppose I just swallowed those fears. They never went away. I just did not put them on public display.

As was always the case, my bus station excursion led to a detention center. Noisy and raucous and raw and violent, I knew what to do in those detention centers. I had developed a look that said despite my size and apparent innocence, leave me alone or suffer the consequences. By then, I was a veteran of those places, and it showed. The bullies knew not to approach me, that they could not terrorize me. The newly initiated would stay away, knowing somehow I was not about to help them swallow their fears or comfort them. My look said there is nothing you can do to frighten me, bully me, or coerce me into doing anything. It was a look that said you are all amateurs when it comes to bullying or suffering. Leave me alone. That look, worn, hard, and calloused, is a valuable currency in those detention centers.

My mother, of course, was no stranger to picking up her children at detention centers. She had developed the well-tuned act of the harried-but-loving-and-worried mother who is inundated with anxiety. My mother could put on a performance that would warm the hearts of even the most jaded social worker. She knew how to evoke deep pools of sympathy for herself, burdened as she was with this horrible child. My mother never tired of that performance, as much as she had to do it, not just for me but for my sisters as well.

She gave a bravura performance when she came to pick me up the next morning to take me back to Cahokia. But with her latest performance over and the curtain down, back in Cahokia she became her poisonous self immediately. She welcomed me back with a hard, scouring, and hot Lysol bath. It stung and hurt beyond belief. I can still smell the antiseptic harshness of that bath. My mother was not afraid of much. Narcissists rarely are. They are so caught up in themselves and their self-absorbed work that they don't have time for fears, I think. But my mother was petrified of germs. After time on the road, with only that brief respite of the bath in the apartment, I was certainly not the cleanest child. My mother was a monster. Was she trying to cleanse her own sins with that hot scouring?

It was clear from my first day back that it would be more difficult to run this time. First, my mother had her meal ticket back, and she was not about to lose that again. With me under her care, she could once again get her precious checks. The always-dutiful and always-cowering Ed boarded up the windows, nailing plywood sheets over them. If the neighbors reacted, I certainly did not hear about it or see it. Neighbors generally stayed as far away from my mother as possible. If she said anything, I'm sure my mother would have reminded the neighbors that I was a runaway. It didn't really matter. She did not care what the neighbors thought.

After she felt I was sufficiently clean, our reunion was not spent in blissful conversation and loving pledges to never let that happened again. My mother took me right down to the courthouse to register that she was once again in charge of me. I was the evidence, right there in flesh and blood. The checks would soon be flowing once again. That was all that concerned her. All this, to me anyway, did not matter a bit. I began immediately to make plans to leave again.

I was back in school in a matter of days, but even as sporadic and uncomfortable as school had been with our frequent moves, this time was different. My struggles had aged me. I looked much older than my classmates. Why would I not? None of them had been through what I had. We no longer had the shared experiences of young girls so vital to friendship.

I felt different, too. I felt the weight of the ages after what I had been through, and it was crushing. I no longer shared the outlook and the innocence of my classmates, and they instinctively knew that. They stayed away from me. I was not welcome. My loss of innocence was too great a gap. I was not the same Betty Rose. I tried, at least briefly. I had so much wanted things to be normal, and I wanted to fit in, to live the life an eleven-year-old should live.

The teachers seemed fine. They seemed to try to help me fit back in. There was, of course, no way for them to know what I had been through. It would have been incomprehensible. I doubt teacher training included units on rape counseling or homelessness for seventh graders.

In terms of classes, I was even further behind, especially in math. It was really a fruitless journey, going back to school. I made it a week, but the pull of running, the desire to remove myself from my mother and her bile, was simply too much to fight. I didn't want to fight it. I wanted to be away once again. The entire time I was back in Cahokia was beyond hell. For one thing, Ed was no longer my uncle. Now he was my stepfather. How Ed and my mother pulled that off in that close-knit community I will never know.

On the first day of my second week back, a Monday, I went to the school office and told the secretary I was feeling terrible and needed to leave. I told them my mother was out and that I would call a family friend for a ride home. In those days, that was a fairly simple thing to do. And the school office wanted as little to do with my mother as possible. Not having her come to pick me up was fine.

I called the father of my best and only friend in Cahokia, Kathy Branscombe. The Branscombes were as close to a real, loving, laughing family as I had ever known. Kathy's parents were the only ones I ever knew who saw through my mother, who recognized and understood her vile and odious personality, her hatred for everything.

The Branscombes were a source of comfort to me on the exceptionally rare occasions I could be with them. I had not seen them in months and had not told Kathy too much of anything that had happened to me, other than it was the worst time I had ever had. Kathy knew enough about me to never pry. I'm sure she must have told her parents that I was suffering. The Branscombes had always been afraid, I think, that one day my mother would eventually break me down, and they always tried to help.

Mr. Branscombe came to the school office immediately. He was a kind man, and it was easy and comforting to read in his eyes the sympathy he had for me. I think if it had been possible, the Branscombes would have adopted me.

Mr. Branscombe brought me from the school to their large and comfortable house. That morning I met a family friend of theirs, Virgil, a sweet nineteen-year-old who was immediately sympathetic to my pleas to not have to go home to my mother. I liked Virgil quickly and felt relaxed enough with him to tell him of my recent time on the road, my visit in Peoria, and my stop at the bus station.

He seemed drawn to me and my troubles and seemed to want to help as were the Branscombes who listened silently as I told my story. As I was finishing my tale, predictably, there was a knock on the door. It was the police, sent to the house by my mother. Mr. Branscombe told the police I was no longer at their house, that he thought I might have gone home.

Then we all agreed I would go across the Mississippi ten miles to Saint Louis, where Virgil's aunt and uncle lived. I would stay with this kind couple for as long as I could before my mother would inevitably learn where I was. The Branscombes knew I had to get away as quickly as I could. They knew that if my mother learned where I was, she would drag me back to hell before I could take a deep breath, and they would be powerless to stop her.

My time with Virgil's aunt and uncle was a peaceful respite. I can't remember how long it lasted. I remember only that they were kind and that I slept well. They were Jehovah's Witnesses. I felt comfortable in the large apartment, which was part of what had once been a grand and expansive mansion. Virgil would come and go but stayed long enough to develop a crush on me. He wanted to marry me, not unusual in that time and place. Certainly not odd in my life, as crazy as it was.

In the small world of Cahokia, there are no secrets, and if there is even the slight hint of intrigue, my mother would smell it and seek it out. She eventually found me in Saint Louis; I'm sure by threatening the Branscombes. I knew she would find me, and I was not surprised when she showed up at the Saint Louis apartment and dragged me back to Cahokia.

Virgil came the next day to my mother's house, pleading that he was only trying to help me by taking me to Saint Louis. I can still remember my mother's next words, bizarre, calculating, and yet in her own cruel way, creative. "Why don't you marry her?"

My mother's self-absorption must certainly have kicked into high gear with this hapless young man at her doorstep, wanting to take me away. She seemed pleasantly surprised Virgil would want to marry me. I'm sure she was imagining a way that I'd be off with Virgil and she would still get her checks. It was a cake-and-eat-it-too scenario, and that was her forte. What would be better?

Virgil and I had shared a friendship, nothing more. We had not even held hands. We certainly did not exchange even the faintest of intimacies. But somehow in Virgil's mind, we were a couple, this very naïve boy and the twelve-year-old girl so much older than her years. I did not want to marry him, if I could even understand the concept at all.

Because I was only twelve, and this was both the 1960s and the South, so it was not bizarrely out of place, people actually considered the marriage of a twelve-year-old not uncommon. But it still required a judge's approval.

It is impossible to try to understand how my mother's mind worked. It was far too impenetrable, and I doubt even the most skilled psychiatrist would be capable of understanding. My mother's rhyme and reason did not fit any scheme, plan, or textbook description.

She wanted to get rid of me and still get her check. The first step was the courthouse in Bellville to file a petition to allow me to marry. She was prepared to sign me away. She was evil. She told the judge in a brief appearance that I was uncontrollable, I was violent, and I incorrigible. Marriage would help, she said. Marriage would be a good thing for me. The judge's decision was clear. No.

My mother was at first appalled that her plans had crashed and burned. After the judge ruled that her fantasy would not happen, she did what she always did. She became angry at me, screaming outside the courthouse that I had once again ruined her life, that I was a curse she would have to bear forever.

Virgil was disappointed. As my mother screamed at me, he took my hand and led me to his car, then drove me to his parents' house nearby, where I met them for the first time.

Today, all these years later, one would have the impression that parents who wanted their nineteen-year-old son to marry a twelve-year-old would be right out of the backwoods, unsophisticated and unaware. But that wasn't the case. They were both very respectable-looking and proper. In fact, I would say that Virgil's mother looked almost prim; well-dressed, short, and very polite. Virgil's mother had a certain look that said "respectable." But they would not have minded Virgil marrying me.

As we sat in their living room and talked about the marriage and its wonderful possibilities, Virgil's mother took my hand gently.

"You can keep Virgil warm at night," she said.

That was the sign for me and it became clear, it was time for me to go. I left.

I simply walked out the door, once more not knowing for sure where I wanted to go but knowing it would be to my favorite destination, away, somewhere, anywhere else.

My first stop to away was back to the Branscombes' in Cahokia. Whether Virgil's parents had a hand in it or whether my moves by then had become predictable, my mother and Ed were soon at the Branscombes' front door with the police.

Soon, I was once again back in the sordidness of juvenile hall. I might as well have become a permanent guest. It was still dirty and still permeated by the odor of fear and pain. I took no consolation in the fact that it was becoming familiar.

My mother took to her stage again. At a hearing the next day to convince a judge and the social worker that I could not be controlled; I, this young, thin, and apparently unsmiling ninety-pound girl could not be controlled. I was too violent and too dangerous for my mother to keep in check, try and try as she did, making great sacrifices all the while.

I needed constant supervision, she told the judge. Try as she had over the years, she could not control my violent impulses. I needed a controlled situation. I needed to be placed somewhere I would be watched. My mother had successfully convinced a judge to institutionalize my father, and I am sure she had that in mind.

She was so convincing that the social worker who drove me back to juvenile hall warned me that she had a gun and would use it if I tried anything. It is incongruous to imagine a fully grown, trained, and experience woman threatening to pull a gun on a thin and frightened young girl, but that is how convincing my mother could be. The social worker took me back to juvenile hall while we waited for the judge's ruling.

My mother had persuaded him as well with her performance. The next day, I would find myself in the police car on the way to Alton. A new and even darker phase in my life was about to begin.

Fourteen

SAINT LOUIS

I read once that you never step into the same river twice, that it changes continuously as it flows by. That, I suppose, is meant to say that life will always be throwing something different at you, good and bad. I wish that were true. All I had thrown at me was bad.

I was trapped in a whirlpool of violence, cycling from one vicious incident to another, and I rarely had a moment to see the light or to even breathe. It seems to me that stepping into a river might be cleansing, cool, and refreshing. My life was never clean or refreshed. No matter what I did or where I went, there was one constant. Regardless of what happened to me as a young girl, nothing would ever be as bad as my mother's behavior.

Steven, my youngest brother, the baby of our family and the last of my mother's children, came to visit me in Georgia recently. I had not seen Steven in years. We had a bittersweet reunion. It was enjoyable in the way that siblings can bond again over shared experiences; sad because it had taken thirty years to see each other again; and bitter because, of course, we talked about our mother.

Steven, more than any of the other children, bore the full impact of my mother's narcissistic, hateful behavior. We had all fled by the time he came along, and Steven had to absorb the brunt of her hatred and bile with no one else around to deflect her hatred. We both agreed all these years later that nothing that had ever happened to us was worse than what she threw at us. Nothing. My mother's behavior was worse than even my escape from Alton to Saint Louis and what happened in St. Louis.

Life at Alton was a mix of almost-paralyzing boredom and moments of sheer terror. It was not a blend that led to anything resembling peace or rehabilitation, or whatever purpose that warehouse served. Very quickly, almost from the first day, I had made friends with Vicki and did all I could to be with her. She was close to my age, for one thing, a rarity in that place where everyone seemed ancient to me. My friendship with Vicki, or however you might choose to describe our relationship, was skewed, of course. We were two teenage girls thrown into that crazy mix, with its drugged and lethargic population one dose away from a complete stupor.

Even my friendship with Vicki was short-lived. Vicki escaped. And in the short time she was away and free, she had somehow found another escape: heroin. By the time she was found and returned, inevitably to Alton, she was an addict. She was placed in a different cottage on her return, and we never spoke again.

Most of the inmates at Alton were, from the perspective of my young eyes, unapproachable. They were older and near-comatose souls barely able to function, to do even the simplest of things. They would get up, get their daily medications, eat, pass the day in a stupor, and go to bed. They all had lived hard lives and were worn to a nub, barely functioning human beings in a barely functioning institution. People at Alton were simply processed and maintained. They were certainly not washed with kindness or any form of useful therapy that might have helped them escape their private hells.

A Mother's Love

With Vicki sequestered in a separate cottage while she recovered, I soon became friends with another girl, a teenager from Saint Louis who was, I guess, much worldlier than I, despite what I had already gone through. Try as I might, I cannot remember her first name. Her surname was Williams. I suppose that memory lapse is natural, considering what she introduced me to, a situation that was so violent and disturbing that it has taken me a lifetime to even think about, let alone try to describe.

Compared with the other residents at Alton, we were close in age, though we had little in common. She was a black girl from the projects of Saint Louis. I was a habitual runaway, a young girl looking for love, friendship, and kindness. Ours was a friendship of convenience, not of shared dreams.

With us during the day was another young black girl named Mary. The three of us formed an unholy trinity I guess. We stayed together as much as we could, with the older and calculating Williams girl leading us along. We followed her direction, as any younger girls would. It was a skewed friendship for sure.

The Williams girl had only one objective, only one thing she spoke about: Going home and being with her boyfriend. Mary and I listened to her lament of missing love and the comforts of home. Mary and I were lured into the dream. I had never had anything close to something I could call home, and the way the Williams girl spoke of her mother and her grandmother and her boyfriend's caring and uninterrupted attention, the better it all sounded. A boyfriend and a place called home, a family to go to. We listened from our own uncomfortable worlds, and it actually sounded magical.

One afternoon, it simply happened. Someone left a door open, a nurse was in another room, and no one else was paying attention. We did not make some grand calculated plan and pull it off in desperation. We just walked out the door, the three of us. We crossed the rolling front lawn and stepped calmly out the front gate.

I was not concerned about racism or racial tension. I wasn't even aware of it. I didn't see black and white. I just saw a young girl close to my age I could talk to. Saint Louis was and still is for that matter a city where segregation was welcomed with open arms. It was tense. I knew tension, and I knew violence. What I did not know as the three of us worked our way down the road to Saint Louis was that I was about to step into more violence than I had ever known, more than I would ever know again. I was lucky to get out alive.

I cannot imagine how they must have viewed me when I walked into the apartment with the Williams girl and Mary. I was a small, brown-eyed white girl suddenly and mysteriously thrust into their grim world. I image they viewed me as insignificant, certainly. Perhaps not as insignificant as my mother always looked at me, but still in a category where I could be easily viewed as nothing.

The apartment building I so innocently stepped into was an angry, enclosed world. I knew nothing of the social implications of crossing the line. But when I did, I was nothing more than an object to be used and discarded like a dirty rag, something to be used, torn apart, and discarded.

After we walked so calmly away from Alton, we had flagged down a bus on the highway. The Williams girl was intent on going home to be with her boyfriend, and Mary and I were swept along. We were soon at the front door of the apartment building in what people in those days called the ghetto, where the boyfriend's mother lived. I was not afraid. I was not anything, actually. I was just there.

The building, a large, old red-brick house, was something that I imagine decades earlier had been impressive and in what was probably an upper-class neighborhood. No longer, though. It was worn and tired-looking and in need of major repairs. We walked through the door and up a short flight of stairs to a small apartment where the boyfriend's sister also lived with her two small children. The children, no more than one or two-years-old, played on the worn linoleum floor.

The comfort from the warmth, the brief relief I felt about being out of Alton, was fleeting. As I sat in a beat-up reclining chair in the corner, I soon became aware that everyone in the room was staring at me. I realized very quickly that those stares bore down on me with more than a hint of hostility. Even the young children were somehow innocently aware that this blond girl in the chair was like nothing that had ever lived in their world. I also knew that there was no escape.

The Williams girl and her boyfriend, after a joyous, shrieking greeting, soon left me and Mary alone with the hostile group; the boyfriend's sister, her children, and several men. They began talking to one another as if I were not there, questioning why I was there and what they should do with me. The discussion was bizarre, obscene, and frightening.

I was trapped. I was alone and powerless. And I was about to be thrown into a ceaseless, violent world of angry men who would tear me apart that afternoon so terribly, so completely, that it has taken me fifty years to bring memories of that day close enough to the surface that I can write about it.

I buried that afternoon for decades, and bringing it back into the light, it comes to me only in flashes, as if I'm watching a horror movie starring myself watching myself. Parts of the show are faded, and others are totally dark.

I remember the Williams girl coming back into the sister's apartment and grabbing me by my collar. I remember her leading me up three flights of stairs to what was a refinished attic apartment, empty except for an old mattress on the splintering wooden floorboards, several dilapidated stuffed chairs, and a large and angry group of men. There could have been as many as ten, or there could have been as few as three. Numbers don't matter.

I remember them passing a bottle among themselves. I see flashes of long, chugging pulls from the bottle, and I hear the obscenities. A wood-burning stove fought to ward off the morning chills.

I can still feel the burning liquor they forced down my throat, one man holding my shoulders while a second forced my mouth open as a third poured the brown, vile, and potent liquor down my throat. I can still feel it coursing up my nose, and I can remember choking.

In a way, that liquor was a saving grace. I passed out, and the rest of the afternoon comes to me only in staccato bursts. Men on top of me, almost suffocating me, grunting. Men tearing at my clothes. Men laughing.

I remember the mustiness and the smells of violence, the men's bodies, and the acrid liquor-scented breath as they came at me on the fetid mattress. One after another. I felt nothing. I was numb. I was surviving again. That is what I had learned to do. Block it out and survive.

I have a brief flash of the silent Mary coming into the room and staring, open-mouthed in shock, then leaving quickly.

The memories become a bit clearer from the point where I can still, even today, see the door of that liquor-filled chaotic attic swinging open. The room becoming suddenly silent as the men started at the grandmother who stood in the doorway with a pistol pointed into the room. She was angry and seething, screaming at what she had seen.

It was very clear that the pistol was not a prop. It was apparent even to me that she would use it if she had to.

"I'll shoot every one of you!" she screamed.

At her side was the boyfriend's sister. Together they pushed aside the crowd of drunken men, pulled me from the mattress, and brought me naked downstairs to the apartment I had so innocently walked into hours before.

There, they put me in a bathtub and drew some warm water. I was numb as the water washed away the physical remnants of that horrid afternoon. The psychological debris will never wash way. I simply and quickly buried it.

The grandmother and sister bathed me and gave me clothes to replace the ones that still lay in the attic, torn and bloody. My new clothes were incongruous: a green miniskirt and a pair of shoes with large shiny buckles. But they were clothes.

They made some spaghetti and covered it with a jar of heated Ragú. I ate mechanically, saying nothing. They had saved my life.

I have no doubt I would have been killed that afternoon. I was not overwhelmed with gratitude, as I recall. Nor was I elated at being given another chance. I was without anything vaguely resembling human feeling or emotion. I let them bathe me, dress me, feed me. I was beyond caring about anything.

The sister and grandmother took me to the bus station and gave me ten dollars. I bought a ticket to Cincinnati and made my way to my father's house. I had nowhere else to go.

Fifteen

FASSAD'S SCHEMES

After Fassad's ill-fated stab at becoming a rock-and-roll hero with his bar and our unceremonious departure from Houston, we bought a ramshackle house near Atlanta and turned it into a home where I could care for elderly patients. My grandmother had told me that elder-care was guaranteed money. Fassad loved guaranteed money, especially if I would be doing all the work.

Fassad used his energy and skills to help renovate the place and get it up to code. It was the last work he would do for quite a while. Fassad told me it was my turn to step up to the plate. Fassad's rules were steadfast.

There is nothing pleasant about Alzheimer's. It is insidious and moves slowly, so those on the outside can watch the gradual erosion. As it progresses, Alzheimer's claims the minds of those unfortunate to be caught in its grip. At first, maybe it's nothing more than "Where are my car keys?" But over time, these seemingly inconsequential moments are replaced as the victim slides into what must be a private hell. They forget to bathe, or shave, or change their clothes. Then they begin to forget where they are, and the worry sets in. Am I losing my mind? What is happening?

A Mother's Love

Soon enough, they will forget to eat, and in the end, they live in what must be a complete vacuum, where nothing gets in or out of their private hell. It must be a horrible way to go. I know this because I've spent much of my life caring for patients with Alzheimer's and other forms of dementia. It is hard work. Physically, a caretaker must lift, clean, and be on constant alert. Emotionally, it is more difficult, as you watch a living and breathing person descend into nothingness.

Sometimes when I look back, I think it might be a pleasant way to spend my final years. I would just ask to be able to keep one memory that sustains me even today, the early years with Allen.

Those first years with the baby were nothing short of perfect. Even the unpredictable Fassad was taken in by the beauty and innocence of that baby boy. Being with Allen, loving him, and having him with me and caring for him was pure bliss. It was everything I had dreamed of and everything I had ever wanted, someone to love who would love me back unconditionally. We bonded the instant I picked him up as he nestled in Fassad's arms on the couch, nursing gently from the bottle Fassad had made for him.

As Allen and I bonded, my uneasy and unpredictable ride with Fassad began to unravel. We would divorce, then remarry. We would fight, then drop back into an uneasy truce. We would leave each other and return. It seemed neither of us could live without the other. Opposites attract, they say, and we were a textbook example.

As our predictable instability continued, several truths emerged. Fassad was incapable of admitting he was in love with me. He would yell that he wanted to get as far from me as possible. But I could not say the same thing to him. He was extremely jealous, and if I so much as talked to a neighbor, he would have a tantrum. Yet, he could not seem to stay away from me. Our lives together after Allen came to us were a chaotic mix of screaming and uneasy peace.

At the center of those days were two constants. First, we both loved Allen. I was a completely doting mother, totally enraptured by this young and beautiful baby boy. Fassad was a strong and distant father who, as he always did, loved Allen in his own way. Maybe that is why Fassad continued to stay with me in our uneasy peace.

The second constant in those years that frightened me and kept me on edge was Fassad's gradual but clearly escalating rage at what was happening to his homeland. American soldiers were in Iraq and killing his countrymen during the first Gulf War. Fassad would watch CNN continuously as coverage of scud missiles hitting his country and killing his compatriots drove him close to the edge, perhaps over the edge at times.

For someone who had come to love America and all the opportunities it had given him, Fassad remained a staunchly rabid and patriotic Iraqi. There was no middle ground for understanding the complexities of what was happening. Fassad lived in a black-and-white world. When I expressed my sympathy for the young American soldiers putting their lives on the line, it would send Fassad into rages that could last for hours. Fassad was a walking time bomb, and his instability was fed by the twenty-four-hour television coverage of the daily destruction.

His anger toward the war would inevitably turn to me, and I would face him, barely able to breathe, hoping he would calm down. Blessedly, thankfully, Fassad would never turn his anger toward Allen. He loved Allen, and I would see, deep down, that Fassad had hidden somewhere a gentleness he preferred hidden, or was incapable of showing. It was that gentleness toward Allen that kept me hoping we would find peace at some point.

Fassad could wreak his own destruction, like the Americans tearing up Baghdad. One evening as the scuds rained down on Baghdad, he jumped from the couch, pulled a file cabinet from the corner of the living room, ripped out its drawers, and began tearing everything to shreds, the files and eventually the cabinet itself, stomping on it and smashing the remnants into the doorframe.

He was not, of course, even remotely concerned about the destruction of our own unstable lives together. He never was. I would learn later from Fassad's brother that Fassad had always been like that, a ticking bomb waiting for the right stimulus to explode. Fassad's brother, a doctor who lived in California, would tell me Fassad was bipolar, which would account for his wild and unpredictable mood swings. That would make sense later. But it did not help our lives together when Allen was a toddler in Georgia and Fassad and I lived in an uneasy truce while I tried to hold things together at our nursing home.

Eventually, I gave up. The United States and Iraq by that time had reached a truce of sorts, but Fassad and I could not. I had to get out. I had had enough. As the war progressed, Fassad stopped working. He was obsessed with the war and its destruction of his country. So devastating was the invasion to him that he stopped the one thing that had driven him ever since I met him: making money as fast as he could and as much of it as possible, no matter how he did it or how many people he took advantage of.

I had no ties to Georgia. I had no ties to anywhere, actually. By then, my work at the home was consuming me, both emotionally and physically. It exhausted me. Fassad liked the arrangement, though, because he no longer had to work and could spend all his time screaming at the television. I soon came to realize my experience and skill that some would call a touch, a gift for caring, was something I could use anywhere.

I convinced Fassad to sell the home, even though we took a loss on it. By then, he was oblivious to what was going on. I took what money I could, packed the car and Allen, and drove way. I wanted Allen to be free of the tension, and I wanted a new start. I had spent my entire life hoping for a new start. I had moved to

Houston hoping to begin afresh, but that only led me to Fassad. Having Allen had renewed my energy, and I sought another new start, this one without Fassad.

That energy would lead me to Sioux Falls, South Dakota. To this day, I cannot tell you why I ended up there. Perhaps because it was as far as I could get from Fassad and the craziness of our lives. Perhaps because I had read that Sioux Falls was the best place in the entire country to raise a family. When I arrived there and found a comfortable place for Allen, I could see why. Sioux Falls was awash in Midwestern sensibilities I had not seen anywhere else in my many travels.

A city of about one hundred thousand people, it was pleasantly different from the rawness of Houston and the impersonal sameness of Georgia. The city was pretty, almost gentle, and it was comfortable. The people were friendly, unhurried, and courteous and seemed concerned. I liked it immediately. But the inevitable intervened.

Allen quickly began to miss Fassad and would cry for him. Fassad quickly began to miss me. He followed me to Sioux Falls. As only he could manage, he did not arrive contritely, expressing his love for me and our son. He arrived angry, screaming at me for choosing such a small and remote place to live. How could I have done that? he asked. Why? he demanded. I knew we would be leaving Sioux Falls soon after Fassad arrived, and we did.

My long drive to Sioux Falls and Fassad's long drive to reclaim our life together triggered a new and peripatetic existence for our young family. We would become gypsies in a way, making long drives to live in various temporary homes in an uneasy peace. Allen held us together. Or at least our common love for that wonderful baby boy held us together. My drive to Sioux Falls seemed to have shaken Fassad from his war-induced rage. His temporarily dormant knack for making fast money came alive again after Sioux Falls. His angry stupor over what Americans were doing to his countrymen was replaced by his keen sense that there was always money to be made somewhere.

For Fassad, it became antiques, or perhaps it was other people's perceptions about what made something antique. Fassad quickly put the two together and just as rapidly found a way to relieve people of their money. He discovered very fast that there was a motherlode of furniture and other items sitting in the barns in Wisconsin and Minnesota that could be purchased extremely cheaply. Then with a truck and his usual sleights of hand, these old worn-out pieces of junky furniture no one wanted up north would be transformed almost magically into rare antiques by the time we got to Georgia.

Even I had to admit it was a stroke of genius. Fassad could unload for a great deal of cash a truck full of old furniture in the course of two weekend days at his roadside "rare antique estate" sales. No one seemed to notice these one-of-a-kind sales seemed to occur every month. To make sure he got as much money as he could by ratchetting up the perceived value of this old furniture, Fassad took to selling them at auction.

Greed loves an auction. The thought that you are outbidding someone always trumps common sense. Word spread quickly. Fassad knew that. By the end, with careful advertising, Fassad could entice more than a thousand people to one of his rare antiques auctions. He was a master of deception. He was back in the mix again at the height of those auctions, raking in the money, being Fassad. He enjoyed separating people from their money. With the antique auctions, there was plenty of money.

Nothing else changed. I knew by then nothing would. We would drive to the upper Midwest, scour old barn sales and rummage sales, then return to Georgia and unload them. Fassad would make a pile of money. We would fight. Or we would sit in uneasy silence. Allen would innocently smile at us both. The waters on the surface were smooth, but underneath, the currents were unpredictable.

Fassad was not one for introspection, for looking into those currents. Neither was I. We sat mired in the unspoken truths of our pasts. He did not want to explain his rage at the world. I did not want to unveil my own dark past, the secrets of my childhood and the twisted intrusions of my mother and her wickedness. To do so for either of us would have been too much. It would have torn us apart, even as shattered and fragile as our life together already was.

And so came the terrorizing moment that Fassad put the gun in my hand and tried to force me to pull the trigger. He could no longer live with me. He could not live without me. For him, there was no choice. He was miserable and wretched. Inside, I was, too.

He put the gun in my hand, placed his over mine, put it to his head, and tried to pull the trigger. He would be dead, and I would spend the rest of my life in prison for killing him. That moment of terror hung frozen there as our neighbor came to the front door and told us our dog had gotten free.

Paralyzed by what he had almost done, Fassad put our hands down and released his grip on the gun. He dropped it on the coffee table in front of us and rose from the couch.

He looked at me. "What just happened?" he asked. "How did we get to this place?"

He was asking how we had reached such a point of desperation. I sat numbly on the couch, relieved to be there. Relieved to be anywhere. I would tell him, I thought. The story would have to begin with my mother. After that, perhaps Fassad would understand.

Sixteen

A MOTHER'S LEGACY

My mother died alone from colon cancer in a Cincinnati nursing home on November 20, 2014. She was eighty-six-years-old and worn down from a life of smoking and anger. I wonder from time to time if the anger that consumed Jackie Greer her entire life finally ate her up. When I heard that her heart had failed, I almost smiled. My mother had no heart. She had no soul. She had only hatred.

Most people will recall the date of a parent's passing with wistful sadness and fond memories of a life well-lived. Most people would be filled with gratitude for the unselfish sacrifices their mother had made. Certainly, anniversaries of those days are bittersweet for most people.

There might be a smaller group of disgruntled children filled with anger and resentment that comes rudely to the surface on the date because of bruising from real or even perceived grievances. No parent is perfect, after all. No child is either, for that matter.

When I heard that my mother had died, I felt nothing, neither sadness, nor grief, nor anger, nor resentment. I went on with the day as I did every other day. Even now, I don't look back on November 20 with any feeling or emotion.

But later, I would have days when the memories of my mother returned and burned right through me. They would make it difficult to breathe. I had always thought that when my mother was in a room, she could suck up the last bit of air, could make it difficult for anyone else in the room to do anything. It was almost as if in death she could still manage to pull off that same trick. In a way, I guess that was my mother's parting gift.

By the time she died, I had not seen her in years. I had at least been successful in that one attempt to avoid her evil magnetism. It was ironic in a way that she had died so close to Thanksgiving. If I had been capable of even the slightest emotions about her, I might have even joked that at last I had something to be thankful for. She was gone. But I was not able to do irony or even make a dark joke. I was too numb from too much for too many years.

After she died, scenes would return to me, running from one horror to another in a staccato rush, like an old movie projector gone amok. My violent rape had ruined her wedding. My erratic behavior forced her to take me to Alton and its own special darkness. I was retarded. I was the child from hell. I was worthy of nothing but punishment. I was a seven-year-old whore. I was a monster.

When I heard that she had died, I felt nothing. There was no sadness, or happiness, or anger. There was nothing.

As a young girl, I had trained myself to drop into nothingness, to retreat into myself. I vowed that I would never surrender my sanity to that woman. I never did and won't now. But remembering her in any fashion still pushes me close to the edge. I have to look at it, though, to understand that I am fine. I am solid. I am scarred, yes, but I am alive and well.

A Mother's Love

Jackie Greer's life was an act, and I was nothing more than a stage prop in a horror movie. So were my siblings. None of us escaped. But as the projector plays the movie starring Jackie Greer, I can pick out scenes in which her truly horrid personality jumps out more than the others. And that is saying something, because she calculated how to make every single action have the most devastating consequences.

Her sister Betty Lou once told me that my mother was the meanest person she had ever met in her life. Betty Lou lived a tough and gritty life and had suffered immensely. For her to say that about my mother and her sister speaks loudly. My mother, in her own mind, lived her life as if she was the star in that movie. She felt that everyone was watching her. I'd learn later that is a critical element of someone with narcissistic personality disorder. In her own mind, everyone was watching, and she wanted reactions. Reactions were victories. Bad reactions were the best. Repulsion and panic and fear and cowering were the reactions she prized the most. They were her trophies. I tried to never react, even though it is difficult not to react to a backhand slap. But for my passiveness, I was reserved a special place in her hell.

She loved to walk up quietly behind me and my siblings and punch us or backhand us as she passed. Sometimes she would do nothing, just walk by quietly. Still, my brothers and sisters would jump. My mother loved that especially, to see them jump back for no reason at all, like well-conditioned animals in her twisted laboratory.

Jackie Greer loved setting her children up, creating a false moment of hope. She was a master illusionist, and we fell for it every time. We were hungry for love, and I think if my mother had showed us love for even a short moment, all of us, all of her battered, damaged children, would have forgiven her past tortures. Maybe we all would have been by her bedside in Cincinnati, holding her hand and comforting her as she withered away. But of course that was not the case.

My mother loved the setup, loved the scene where she would approach and put a gentle hand on my back and smile. She would hint that she was about to offer a kind word. I would look up expectantly. Then she would transform herself. She had gotten the reaction, the little sign that I might be hoping she was about to hug me and comfort me.

Then she would follow through with a backhand slap or perhaps try to force her closed fist down my throat. Before I learned to shut down and not feed her hunger for reactions, I never failed to hope, and she never failed to follow through with a crushing blow or some sort of vile and vulgar rant.

After years of that, inside, no matter how well or smoothly things were moving along, I would be startled and nervous, locked out and shut down. People could talk, and I wouldn't hear. My heart raced for no apparent reason. I spent my entire childhood like that.

Years later, it took me twenty-five cents and a yard sale to finally learn what might be behind my mother's machinations. I bought the *Diagnostic and Statistical Manual of Mental Disorders*. The book had opened my eyes to my mother's very real narcissistic personality disorder. But the eye-opening clinical language and descriptions did not come close to the visceral and painful experience of living with her. An academic textbook cannot jump the chasm into the reality of living with someone like Jackie Greer, even though it would be a stretch to call my childhood "living." I survived my childhood. I survived Jackie Greer.

Most casual observers would tell you a narcissist is someone who admires herself beyond normal proportions, someone who needs to have a mirror nearby. But that is only a superficial definition. Narcissists are not capable of love or human emotion. They cannot connect with the outside world. The definition of narcissistic personality disorder is uniquely unflattering:

> *Narcissistic personality disorder is a mental disorder in which people have an inflated sense of their own importance, a deep need for admiration and a lack of empathy for others. But behind this mask of ultraconfidence lies a fragile self-esteem that's vulnerable to the slightest criticism.*

—MAYO CLINIC STAFF

My mother's lifetime goal, a goal she pursued every day, was to divide and separate. She pitted one set of people around her against another. Her children, the neighbors, her own family. It didn't matter as long as she was the center of attention.

My mother beat me. She insulted me with vulgar comments. She excelled at devising creative ways to punish me and my siblings. She was creative. Not reacting was my victory, and I relish that. But the damage was immense. Anyone looking back at the path of devastation in Jackie Greer's life will see a cluttered trail of broken people.

I was a constant source of disappointment to my mother throughout my life, from the moment I was born, I suspect. If I succeeded at something, it would bring out her worst. Graduating from high school, adopting Allen, running my own business, living on my own and thriving, getting married—each of these milestones that would make a normal mother proud only incensed her. They made Jackie Greer sink into her desperate plans to somehow ruin what might pass as my happiness. My success was her worst nightmare. My mother was a monster.

I would learn that a narcissist projects her own greatest fears onto her victims. So her oft-repeated claims that I was a whore who would never amount to anything spoke loudly of what tormented my mother.

I do have to admit she was talented and fooled most people her entire life. She could make up stories so bizarre and unbelievable that people who did not know her would assume that they had to have happened. If anyone had doubts about what she was saying, she would switch gears and threaten. People soon knew it was better to stay away from her and whatever world she lived in. They did not see Jackie Greer waking us every morning by throwing us from bed. They did not hear her daily screaming.

I look back at my life like a rubbernecker at the scene of a horrible accident. I don't want to look, but I can't help it. Scenes come rushing back, and I cannot avert my eyes. The memories are like a violent flood, and I try to keep my head above water. I lived with her words every day.

"I hate you."

"You are a no-good son of a bitch."

"You make me sick."

"I want you dead."

"I don't care what other people say. I am your mother, and I know you're retarded."

"Die so I can finally be free of you."

"Anyone who looks at you knows you are a freak of nature, you little whore."

My mother was a talented actress. People saw us in church, and my mother always brought us to church and put us on display, like little props in her imaginary heart-wrenching world. She wanted everyone to look at the loving and long-suffering mother with the irascible kids she tried to love. She wanted that pity and admiration. She wanted that sympathy. That was worth more than gold to Jackie Greer.

A Mother's Love

She loved strangers. People outside our family circle saw a different Jackie Greer, and for her, that was the way it was supposed to be. That completed the equation, in her demented mind at least. People on the outside were the audience in the movie starring Jackie Greer in which she was the loving, long-suffering mother cursed with ungrateful children and a tough economic situation. She wanted everyone to look at her and think, *She is a wonder. It is marvelous the way she keeps on despite her hellish burden.*

Outsiders did not see her every morning, her constant cigarette hanging from her mouth, enveloping us in smoke as she screamed at us to eat the French toast or pancakes she had worked so hard to cook for us ungrateful wraiths, little no-good, worthless kids.

The breakfast scenes always followed her first ritual of the day, pulling us from our beds and beginning her daily screams. She always scrubbed my face as if she were trying to erase some indelible spots only she could cleanse. Then she brushed my hair roughly and dressed me. She did the same for my siblings. We all sat for breakfast neatly dressed and clean. That was for the public display later. Then she yelled. Every single day began like that.

Jackie Greer hated every one of her children without exception. For me, because I refused to give in, she reserved a special place in hell. I wonder what she thought as she lay in the Cincinnati nursing home, wasting away, if she ever had regrets. Did she ever feel some remorse for her legacy? Did she ever wonder why she was alone at the end?

I doubt it. The film in her mind likely was playing to a melodramatic climax. I suppose as she lay there, in her mind she was the sad and rebuffed mother, the saint dying a saintly death while her ungrateful children ignored her to the end.

As my memories of her sometimes intrude on my life, I can't help but think of her screaming at me after my rapes in Cincinnati that I had ruined her wedding to Ed. I think of her sending me to

Alton as if I were an unwanted package. I think of her visiting me there and looking at the hollow-eyed, drugged-out inmates. When she saw the shuffling vacant shells of those people, did she feel any remorse? If she had regrets about locking me up at Alton, they were more likely about wishing she had done so earlier.

Her last grasp at tormenting me was to reach out after I sued the Houston gynecologist for his lies and botched operation. Her mind was still agile and creative in its ability to think of ways to ruin my life. She had told him to be wary of me, that I would kill him.

That, for me, was one of the last straws. I had not seen her for more than thirty years when she died. Yet she still reaches out and troubles me today, and I cannot help but think of her.

I'm overcome with one thought: How sad for her that she never got to know the kind, caring person I am.

Seventeen

THE FINAL TRIAL

My life is a gift.

It has taken years to reach the point where I can talk about what I have been through, to open the doors I closed so tightly years ago. I shut down as a young girl to survive. I locked up emotions and kept them to myself. Sharing my very real hope that someone, somewhere, at some point would reach out to me was far too painful. Each time I tried, I failed. I never gave up the hope. I just kept it locked tightly in my own private world, where everything was safe, light, and loving.

Along the way, I had hoped someone would rescue me. Living in one's own vacuum is not any way to go through life. At various points along the way, I had hoped my brothers and sisters would offer comfort. Then maybe my father. But they had their own devastations to cope with. My mother was too strong in her hatred and psychological violence. Her control was complete. I would find no solace from family. Jackie Greer was too strong.

I had hoped, briefly, that perhaps the nuns would see a troubled young girl and give me shelter. But nuns know nothing of the real world. I saw love briefly in the Branscombes, but they could not penetrate Jackie Greer's shield. I think I loved Jose in a way. He was sweet and caring. I know he loved me. But alcohol was his first love, and alcohol clouds judgment. God knows I tried. But I had to shut down. It was the only way I could survive.

Those glimpses of love to me were like drops of water to a dying soul trying to cross the Sahara. They were enough to sustain me and keep me going. They allowed me to survive and continue to hope for a never-ending stream of fresh, clean, and life-giving love, somewhere, somehow, from someone.

As hard as it has been to reach the point where I can talk about it, my life was not a barren desert that offered nothing but pain, as twisted and dark as it was many times. My life has given me a strength few people have. Why would they possess such a will? No one would volunteer to pass through the things I have overcome to gain the strength I now have.

I don't wear my strength like an emblem. I don't flaunt it. I don't preach, sermonize, or call the world to my doorstep so they can hear what I've learned. But it is there, that strength, and it is stronger now than it has ever been. And that strength comes at a time when I need it the most. It is there to help the one person I love more than anyone else in the world.

Allen shattered the tight seal I had put on my emotions. He completely and wondrously destroyed what I had so deliberately built around me, the protection I had successfully managed and needed to survive. Allen changed my life. It turns out he was the one person I had been looking for. He was a miracle and in many ways a lifesaver. If I did not have Allen, I would not have managed to survive, I'm sure. I was nothing if not a survivor. Allen allowed me to show everyone I had feelings and was no longer hiding them, cowering and silently and passively waiting for the next blow. Allen made me love and allowed me to show love.

A Mother's Love

Today, I am happily married. I'm successful in business. I have a nice home and live comfortably. I am bedrock solid in my ability to withstand shock. I go with the flow, bending but never breaking.

Life with my mother has pushed me toward perfectionism, which is not necessarily a good thing. I was never good enough for my mother. That branded me with a desire to always be perfect. Perhaps now as I look back, it was a compulsion. I worked hard at every single thing I did. When I was done, I returned and worked harder. I tried to be the perfect mother, to be the mother I never had. In his youth, Allen was the perfect son. He still is in many ways. But there were problems later.

Now, today, Allen is the reason that the strength I have developed over the years will help. Everything I have been through has given me strength that today I share with Allen. He needs it.

Allen came to me like a wonderful gift. He allowed me to love unconditionally for the first time in my life. He allowed me to burst the dam of love I had kept inside my entire life. I had always wondered what love was. Like a stranger in a foreign land, where people had weird customs and an incomprehensible language only they knew, I was an outsider in that world. I wasn't sure what it was, this love. I had heard about it in church, in school, and on TV. But I had never felt it before.

When Allen arrived, I loved him immediately. I adored him from the instant I picked him up from Fassad's sleeping embrace, took the bottle from his mouth, and kissed him. It was a divine moment, that first embrace, and I can feel it still. And in a way, I never stopped that embrace.

In return, Allen gave me something I had never had, an unconditional love. From the instant I held Allen, I knew what life was supposed to be about. I drowned him in the love that I had held inside, locked up, for so long through so many trials, and accepted his in return. Nothing I had been through or would go through after that moment changed a thing.

Today, I wonder and ask myself this question: Is it possible to love too much? Is it possible that I was so drawn from a loveless life that I sucked up too much of it?

These days, I try to see Allen every week. That can be difficult. I look at him, talk to him, encourage him, love him. I try to tell him to keep going. I try with everything I have to fill him with hope. He needs hope. In a way, he needs today to adopt my method of shutting down and waiting for the light. I tell him his situation is temporary, that it will pass.

I look back now and see that all I had been through had prepared me for this. All the crushing blows I had experienced were nothing compared with the pain of seeing such a gentle and loved boy get caught in the evil eddy and be pulled down into the undertow.

Allen is in prison now. He spends each day surrounded by gangs, hopelessness, and the always-present threat of violence. There is not a single person on earth more prepared to help that poor boy now than me. I had been in prison my entire life until I embraced Allen that first time. I had been hopeless. I had retreated into myself to survive, just as he does every day.

I made it through the darkness, and today, I can give Allen the strength to do the same. That is the gift my hard life has proved me with. I give Allen hope. All that I have been through, my trials, have prepared me today to help him. Allen looks forward to my visits and my strength. I want Allen to know my strength, to absorb it like a dry sponge. This woman, his mother, has made it through some very hard times. If he knows that, then I have done my job, and everything I have been through is worth it, every single wretched moment.

That is my gift. My hope, serenity, and strength seem to sustain Allen. He knows nothing of my past. He knows only that I had some tough times. I don't talk about the details. The details would overwhelm him now, at a time when he is already overwhelmed. The details of my life don't matter. Only the strength I have gained matters. I can see each time I visit him that my strength sustains him.

I think back at times to one of my mother's vicious peculiarities. I think about how she would threaten to kill me, then bury me in the backyard. How she would tell me that no one would even know I was gone. I think about how often she would tell me she prayed to God every night for forgiveness for bringing me into the world. She thought I was contaminated with germs and would tell me that every day. I was never allowed to stand close to someone else's food or drink.

Odd that those thoughts come back to me now after I had buried them for so long. But today, I want to be contagious. I want to infect Allen with the hope I have earned after such a long, hard life. I made it through the fires of hell and became strong and resistant to despair. And that is my gift to my son.

I've learned much and have seen success. The road to get there was long and tortured, of course, but it prepared me for the great challenge I would face in a lifetime of challenges.

Allen was the perfect child, loving when I needed someone to love. He was obedient and respectful. More than anything, he was kind, curious, and bright. He was nothing short of a perfect child, a blessing I cherished each day. I would look at Allen and know, after a life of being told I was incapable of doing anything right, that I had done something right. I lavished Allen with all the love I could summon, and in return, Allen loved me unconditionally. He was everything I had ever wanted or dreamed of. He was perfection.

Things changed by the time he was fifteen. I had always been prepared for obstacles, of course, but life with Allen to that point had been so smooth and pleasant. Adolescence and the first tentative steps of adulthood challenged Allen, and I was not prepared to fight that battle.

Bettyrose Woody

Allen met a girl, really a woman. She was nineteen and caught up in herself and infatuated by the young boy she could control. I suppose it was inevitable. It was certainly not unusual. A mother's love cannot compete with hormones and a young man's first thirst for independence. God knows I tried. And given the results of what happened and where Allen is today, I certainly try to carefully examine and figure out what I did wrong. I try not to second-guess what today is my greatest challenge in a lifetime of challenges. That is another thing I have learned. Second-guessing is a foolish waste of time, needless wheel-spinning that will get me nowhere. Yesterday is gone. Tomorrow has not yet come. I have only today.

This woman took over Allen's life. His infatuation with her and her way of life completely and totally swept him off his feet. She appeared to be independent, freewheeling, and full of sass, vigor, and sex. She drank. She smoked pot. She thumbed her nose at everyone and everything. She was quite taken with Allen, who at fifteen was a handsome man-child. More than anything, though, he was naïve and malleable. I had made him that way. I had kept him from the rough edges, the disappointments, and the tough spots that had made me so strong. I felt he did not need that sort of training to be strong. Perhaps I should have given him a taste of disappointment. I never did. I never wanted him to know a single second of disappointment. I felt I had had enough of that to last the two of us an eternity. And so it went.

Allen became consumed with that young woman. I had tried to get him away from her by sending him to military school. It was not surprising to me that he did well there, excelled in fact. But by then, he was too smitten. She had total control. When he came home from school on breaks, she was back in his life immediately. His life revolved around her, and that meant drugs and alcohol and all the detritus that goes along with it.

He was intoxicated with her and her melodrama. She thrived on crazy-making. I would try to force separations. They would threaten suicide. I would plead for reason. They would respond with chaos. He would find work, then quit. He would make a stab at doing what a young man should do, but he could never escape her pull.

When Allen was nineteen, he first got into serious trouble, a drug charge along with larceny. He was sentenced to nine months in a detention center. I thought that would scare him, make him reconsider what he was doing and where he was going. But by then, he was too smitten. That detention center was mild compared with where he is now.

When he got out, he was still under the supervision of a probation officer and rules that called for random drug testing. At first, he did well. But she was young and controlling. She was a Svengali who had hypnotized him into submission. Allen loved her. She hovered. It was inevitable that with her around he would fail. And he did. Things escalated. More charges, more stupid attempts to get fast money and more drugs.

I allowed Allen and his new girlfriend to move in with us, thinking I could help. But I could do nothing by watching, like a mute and powerless onlooker. Soon, there were friends over and beer parties and kids hanging around. He quit work. He was soon back on drugs, back with people who dragged him down, swimming in a current that would sweep him inevitably back into trouble. Soon, it was not juvenile detention but jail, then prison, the inevitable course of drugs.

I watched, powerless. It was as if everything passed by in slow, distorted motion that I could do nothing to stop. It was like watching two cars approaching each other at high speed and not being able to stop the massive collision. I watched. I warned. I pleaded.

The union did produce something positive, my grandson, Isaac. I vowed to make sure he never went a moment without knowing he had someone to care for him. It speaks volumes that later, when his mother would return from one of her many unexplained absences that he would run to me for protection.

She has a new man in her life and refuses to let my son and I see Isaac. One of her family members contacted us and said that she was living with a new boyfriend and wants to erase my son and me from Issach's life. She lived with us for several years. She and my son never paid anything for living expenses. They had occasional sporadic employment. They always asked me for money to purchase cigarettes or fast food. She did not like that I tried to have some semblance of rules. I only asked that dishes be washed immediately after a meal, not a few days later; not to take food and drinks into the bedrooms; not to throw cigarette butts on our carport. I did not want teenagers spending the nights drinking or using drugs. I ask that the door stay locked at all times. I also did not like them staying up all night and sleeping all day every day. My son and I were not agreeing on this living arrangement. I thought the house rules were within reason. I had to maintain some control. She resented me and used my grandson to hurt us. We are concerned he thinks that we abandoned him and cause him psychological damage. My son and grandson are my most precious assets. Isaac will always know love as long as he's near me.

One incident sums up her self-absorption and my suspicion she had her own narcissistic demons as well. One night, Isaac was running a high fever. I walked carefully into her room and woke her, saying we needed to take Isaac to the emergency room, that his fever was dangerously high.

"Are you frigging kidding?" she said. "At this hour? I need my sleep."

Allen is now property of the Georgia Department of Corrections. He goes where it sends him. He has some more time to serve. That is where I can help. He has had a tough time in prison, and I make frequent calls to the warden to plead for his safety. He is not a hardened criminal, just someone who was swept into the current. He was not prepared for what he is living today. Hardened prisoners can smell the fear and the lack of preparation.

Allen is having a tough time. Gangs are predatory, and Allen is the perfect victim.

Prisons are hard, rough, and, in Georgia, ruled by gangs, while prison officials look the other way. I continue to try to see Allen as much as I can. Because when I do, I can offer him my strength. I have to stay strong for Allen until he gets out. He looks to me for help and solace. He sees my strength and draws from it. It sustains him. I can see it each time I visit.

I see his downcast eyes lift when I visit. I see how he lights up when he watches me walk in. He smiles his beautiful smile and becomes, if only briefly, the wonderful boy I knew years ago. It is no doubt the only time he smiles during the week. His life is tough and barren and emotion is a sign of weakness. It dawns on me when I look for meaning into all I have been through. This is what it was all about, all the darkness of my life. This is what it was for.

My own trials have given me a gift I can share with my son. Every single dark moment was a seed of hope and strength that poor young man needs. He needs my strength to draw on and stay strong. I never gave up. Now he won't either. He draws strength from me. That's what it was for, to help my son. If that is the case, it was all worth it.

Afterword

Dear Mother,

I did not intentionally ruin your wedding. Janie and I were upset you were marrying Ed and moving us back to Cahokia. We didn't want to leave our family. As long as we lived in Cincinnati, we had their protection from you. I didn't want another beating from you.

I ran and hid in the bushes after you drove through the alley, then I walked around to the drugstore. I had just turned eleven-years-old. The teenage boy asked me if I wanted a ride to Daddy's. After I accepted, he said he wanted to first stop and show me his mother's new carpet. He raped me in her bed. I didn't know what to do. He then drove me to Daddy's. When I looked in the window and saw Grover sleeping, I felt a tremendous amount of shame. I didn't know how to face anyone after what had happened.

But I did not run away. I didn't know how to process these horrible events. You accused me of raping him. You said I was a no-good whore. No matter what happened to me, you always said it was my fault. I was raped, and all you could think about was your wedding. It was always about you.

You had me committed to Alton State Mental Hospital after I was raped. You went before a judge and described yourself as if it were me. That was the only way you could commit me. I know you had a rush of joy, all while you silently applauded yourself for your outstanding performance in court. The adulation you felt.

You were a master of deception. How many times in my life had you blatantly accused me of ruining your wedding because I was a whore? You mocked me and laughed at me. I was a dirty joke in your eyes. You always said I made you sick just looking at me. You said you wished I were dead, that you wanted to kill me and bury me in the backyard. You said no one would ever ask about me. You prayed I would die. You said I was like a green blob that was oozing green slime that repulsed everyone.

You said numerous times that no matter where I went people would find out how despicable I was and hate me. No decent human being would ever want to be with me, you told me. You said I was a freak of nature.

After Ron Knable told you I could no longer stay at Alton, I had to be placed somewhere else. You couldn't take a chance of losing your check. So you had them return me to you. I never told you, but I didn't want to go back with you. I was treated better at Alton than I was by you. For two years, nurses gave me respect and cared for me. Thank God for them. They showed me the love I had never known, love I only dreamed of.

When I was sent back to you, Jenny was the only one who welcomed me. You stood at the kitchen sink as if you didn't know what to do with me. I knew you didn't want me. I always knew that. Janie, your chosen one, was very upset when I came back. As soon as she walked in and saw me, her first words were, "Drop dead, bitch."

You had convinced her that I was contaminated with every germ after living in that hospital. Yes, it was filthy. Even though it might have been possible, I would never intentionally infect Janie and her baby. You always played Janie and me against each other. You accused me of being jealous of her. You would lie to her and tell her things I said that I had not. You created excruciating drama. You loved the rivalry your lies created.

Living with you was not unfamiliar territory. The two babies, Theresa and Dickie, gave me someone to love. I loved the babies, and they loved me. You were pregnant again with Stephen. I had to somehow acclimate you and Janie to having me living there again. I made myself valuable, and before long, I was the babysitter as well. I started cleaning the house, hanging clothes on the line. I did the household jobs no one else wanted. And after that, you still told me to not get close to food that someone was going to eat. Because of those sweet babies, I survived another round with Jackie Greer.

While I was locked away for two years in Alton, you needed someone to torture. So you chose Jenny. Poor Jenny, she didn't know how to handle the constant narcissistic destruction. You were relentless toward her. Jenny was a sweet little girl. She was afraid of everything. You knew exactly how to take one of your children's lives and twist the life into the twilight zone. It wasn't long until you were boarding the windows to prevent Jenny from running away from you. That's exactly what you did to me. You shaved Jenny's head and tied her to a chair so she wouldn't try and escape from you.

You tortured Jenny with dolls, Janie with spiders, and me with knives. Although Janie was the chosen one, she didn't completely escape your abuse. When Jenny finally left, you blamed me over and over. You said I had a demon that left me and went to Jenny. You never took responsibility for the evil destruction you caused us. Jenny left because she could no longer live with your sadistic abuse. That's why Jenny moved into the rectory with the priest. He rescued her from you. But the mental damage you inflicted on Jenny could never be reversed. Another stellar performance. You broke poor Jenny. You left her a mental case she will never recover from. You were a monster.

As long as I lived with you, the abuse was directed at me. I was the black sheep, as you told me over and over. I hated the abuse, but I was stronger than Jenny and Stephen, even Daddy. I refused to surrender my sanity to you. I can still smell your cigarettes from when you would wake me in the mornings. I can still hear your screaming, "You no-good, dirty son of a bitch! Get your lazy ass out of that bed."

You would say that the fact that I was alive and breathing made you sick. How you hated me and wanted me dead. You would ask God to kill me.

You directed Janie and me to attack Jenny, and we did. We did not want to hurt Jenny. I will regret that for the rest of my life. We were all desperate to please the monster. So we beat Jenny up in the street while you stood and instructed us as to what to do. The neighbors just watched. You were so damn evil.

All we wanted was your love, and we would have done anything for it. Not a single one of your children will ever know a mother's love. At night, you would go outside and beat on the windows and doors to frighten us or walk into a room and start screaming to watch the fear drain calmness from our faces. You loved our fear, and you adored yourself for inflicting it on us.

You laughed at us. And your daily naps, oh my God, how did we survive those? You were at your worst for those naps, at the height of your evilness. God in Heaven knows no one made a sound, not when the monster took a nap. You would wake up and walk in, cursing me, swearing, beating me, punching me, dragging me around the house by my hair. You were delusional. You kept beating me, demanding that I cry.

You used my hair to anchor your grip as you banged my head into the wall. Hell, I was determined not to give you the satisfaction of seeing me cry. I would rather you beat me than give you a reaction. Later, you would call me and describe to me how you beat me. You would laugh and compliment your strength. I knew what you wanted, and I wasn't going to give it to you.

You could yank my hair out of my head until I was bald, and you'd give yourself a medal. Every day, I listened to you curse me for living. But after a while, it didn't mean anything to me anymore. I got to the point where what you said didn't matter to me.

I was concerned for my siblings only. I knew you were a witch. You had everyone living in fear of you, and no one would cross you. You accused me of having a big mouth that told everything, but that was also a lie. If I told everything you did, you would have been in the penitentiary years ago. You accused me of what you were.

A Mother's Love

Every day you cooked. Dinner was at five o'clock, and the only way we could miss dinner was being dead. While you prepared dinner, you screamed how you slaved over a hot stove to cook for us no-good, ungrateful bastards. Every day, you would do and say the same thing as you cooked.

You would call me in the kitchen and pretend like you were going to stab me or cut me with the knife. That thrilled you. You would make stabbing motions with it, then turn it quickly so the handle would hit my chest. You did this every day, even if I was holding a baby.

Your long stories were all lies. In those stories you were always the sweet, helpless victim who was taken advantage of. You said you were the only reputable person in your family. You said your mother wanted to discredit you, starve you, and tell outlandish lies about you. You told of how your mother would rob people, how she sold her soul to the devil so she could gain riches from robbing old people who lived at one of Grandma's nursing homes. You lied about your sister Betty Lou, the sister you hated, the sister you named me after. You abused Betty the same way you abused us. Betty Lou told me you also tried to stab her and shove your fist down her throat, just the same way you did me. You lied about Betty numerous times over the years. Thank God Betty Lou had Grandma to protect her. I had no one.

I asked Betty Lou why no one had ever checked on us. She said they never thought you would torment your children the way you had. They knew you were evil, but they didn't know how deep your evilness was. Betty told me how you had difficulties when you were young. Betty Lou was the only person who did not fear you. She told me Grandma wanted to protect you. They knew what you were. You also hated your sister Katie. You accused Katie of robbing Grandma. You said Katie changed Grandma's records. Katie was lucky she was born only a few years before you married Daddy. She escaped most of your evilness, but she wasn't completely spared.

You hated both of your brothers. You stole Daddy away from his wife, Jean. You turned that narcissist charm on Daddy, and he didn't know how to resist you. Daddy was just another challenge for you. And a married man made it more exciting. Daddy made a grave mistake hooking up with you. You got pregnant. You were going to have Daddy either way.

You had the baby, a baby you refused to love or care for. Poor Danny was neglected more than any of your children. I cannot understand how a woman can have a child and literally hate and reject that baby. Danny's life has been bleak.

A narcissistic woman can mesmerize any man. even a happy, married man with three children. I know how charming you were because I saw you in action. You once said Jean Woody didn't want Daddy or any other woman to have him. My half brother David told me how devastated Jean was when Daddy left her for you. Jean wanted Daddy. David also said his mother confronted you and asked you to step away from Daddy. He was with her when she went to see you at work. My God, it hurt me that Janie had done that, and it still hurts me to this day.

While I was there, I spent time with Grover. He was angry at the abuse you inflicted on him. Because of what had transpired earlier with Janie, I wasn't completely able to absorb it all. Grover at that time hated you. I sat with him for hours. He described your wicked behavior. He told me how you screwed around on Daddy in Daddy's bed. He described in detail what you had done to him, Daddy, and Danny.

Grover warned me to stay away from you because you would terrorize my household. I said, "Grover, I just want Mom to love me."

He said you were not capable of loving anyone. All you would do was hurt me. He told me how you put him and Danny in an orphanage, then gave them to Daddy.

I said, "Mom always said you and Danny didn't want her."

He told me they wanted you, but you didn't want them. I should have listened to my older brother, but I didn't. I thought somehow, someway I would earn your love, but it never happened.

You terrorized my life, and you know what you did. For twenty-seven years, you didn't know what had happened to me. I talked to no one. Van found me after you died. I asked Van if you had ever asked about me, and he said, "No. Never."

Van gave me Stephen's and Theresa's telephone numbers. I called them both immediately. I talked to Theresa for hours. I asked her, "Did Mom ever ask about me?"

She said, "No. Never."

Stephen called me, and a few months later, he moved here. Stephen was a broken man and physically sick with cancer and multiple sclerosis. Cancer had metastasized throughout his body. He did not tell me everything, but he said enough. He described your wickedness. He was the last child to live with you. So you gave it all you had. He was the finality of your meanness. He did tell me how you would scream that you knew he was a queer and had sex with men.

He wasn't a queer or retarded. Stephen was a genius. He said he had left for ten years and Van had found him. Stephen was in love with a beautiful woman named Katrina. He told Van he would never take someone he loved near you.

You wanted to destroy all your children. Stephen had reminded me of how you would insist we play the Ouija board. I had forgotten how psychic you were until Stephen. Stephen told me when he and Theresa were young, they prayed every day that I would come and keep them for the weekend, just for a rest from you. He also said that if it wasn't for me, he would never have known love or kindness. All you could give was an iron fist.

Stephen died here at home with me. There was no way I would let him stay with strangers to die. My husband, Joe, was with him when he took his last breath. I was on the telephone talking to Theresa when he passed.

Van is the only one who escaped your wickedness. You gave him some but not on the same level as us. Van just described you as a house of horrors. He said very little about anyone. Van is just like Daddy. He's happy and loves everyone in his family. Van is a good guy. Van is a lucky guy.

Mamma, I am very sorry that you had such a hard life growing up. Growing up during the Depression had to be difficult. I am sorry for whatever caused you to be the way you were. Whatever it was, it stole everything from you. You were just a young child with the responsibility of your siblings, and you had no food to eat. Your father was gone, and your mother was working.

Mamma, I have tried to hate you, but I can't. You had serious issues. It wasn't your fault. I can only empathize with what your life took from you and all of us. It stole our mother and gave us a monster. I am sorry that I disappointed you. I only wanted to please you. If I had known you were dying, I would have gone to see you.

I don't blame you for anything. I apologize for anything I ever did that disappointed you or angered you. I myself have made many mistakes throughout my life. I love you and forgive you, and please forgive me.

Love,
Bettyrose

Made in the USA
Columbia, SC
30 December 2017